CLEARING THE HAZE

CLEARING THE HAZE

Helping Families Face Teen Addiction

Christian Thurstone, MD, and Christine Tatum

ROWMAN & LITTLEFIELD
Lanham • Boulder • New York • London

Published by Rowman & Littlefield
A wholly owned subsidiary of The Rowman & Littlefield Publishing Group,
Inc.
4501 Forbes Boulevard, Suite 200, Lanham, Maryland 20706
www.rowman.com

Unit A, Whitacre Mews, 26-34 Stannary Street, London SE11 4AB

British Library Cataloguing in Publication Information Available

Library of Congress Cataloging-in-Publication Data

Thurstone, Christian.
Clearing the haze: Helping families face teen addiction / by Christian Thurstone, MD, and Christine Tatum.
 p. cm.
Includes bibliographical references and index.
ISBN 978-1-4422-3105-4 (cloth : alk. paper) -- ISBN 978-1-4422-3106-1 (electronic)
1. Teenagers--Substance use. 2. Substance abuse--Treatment. 3. Addicts--Rehabilitation. 4. Ad-
dicts--Family relationships. I. Tatum, Christine. II. Title.
RJ506.D78T48 2015
616.8600835--dc23
2014049997

∞ ™ The paper used in this publication meets the minimum requirements of
American National Standard for Information Sciences Permanence of Paper
for Printed Library Materials, ANSI/NISO Z39.48-1992.

Printed in the United States of America

For our children—Tatum and Asa—and yours.

CONTENTS

Foreword   ix
Patrick J. Kennedy

1 Why Adolescent Substance Use Is a Big Deal   1

2 Parents' Tools for Planning, Communicating, and Monitoring   19

3 What to Do When You Learn Your Child Is Using Drugs   39

4 When to Seek Treatment and What to Look For in It   53

5 Specific Family Objectives during Treatment: The Theory   71

6 Specific Family Objectives during Session: The Practice   89

7 How Parents Can Help Their Adolescents Not Use Substances   99

8 Addiction Is a Chronic Condition That Requires Chronic Maintenance   111

9 Taking Care of You   119

10 Advocating for Adolescent Substance Prevention   129

11 Additional Resources   139

12 Summary   145

Bibliography   151

Notes   159

Index   167

About the Authors   171

FOREWORD

Patrick J. Kennedy

I am no stranger to mental health issues and addiction. I have struggled with bipolar disorder and addiction in a family that, like many, is affected by mental health and addiction in a country where more than sixty million people suffer from these problems.

There is no health without mental health. There is no checkup without a checkup from the neck up! The brain is not only the most important part of our bodies, it's the very essence of our soul, creativity, and ability to connect.

We are all affected by mental health issues and addictions in one way or another. Unfortunately, lack of access to treatment and the stigma associated with mental health and addiction remain too common. Not to mention, mental health research is woefully underfunded.

In a world in which all of us would benefit from "whole health," too many people with mental illness or addiction go without treatment. Efforts to improve care and accelerate brain research will help not just our fellow countrymen, but all people across the globe. Everyone benefits when we protect the most precious resource we possess—our brains, especially the brains of our youth.

I was chief sponsor of the 2008 Mental Health Parity and Addiction Equity Act (MHPAEA). This legislation requires group health insurance plans to provide mental health and substance abuse coverage equivalent to their coverage for physical health. I cofounded One Mind (www.onemind.org), whose mission is to accelerate open science and advance research that has made great strides in these areas. As the guardian of MHPAEA, I have also founded The Kennedy Forum (www.thekennedyforum.org) to both advance parity and set the standard for best practices going forward.

This book shows parents and families how to navigate the dangerous waters of adolescent addiction. You will find Dr. Thurstone in many places: he is providing care to youth, advising professional athletes and soldiers, discussing mental health and addiction with state and federal lawmakers, and conducting research. He stands out as a distinguished clinician, researcher, and advocate with a passion for promoting accurate information and quality mental health care. This book provides reliable information in determining if there is a problem, where to turn for help, and how to help yourself, your child, or a loved one.

This is the civil rights issue of our time. We are all stakeholders in the race to inner space, and Dr. Thurstone is helping to lead the way.

I

WHY ADOLESCENT SUBSTANCE USE IS A BIG DEAL

Every year, people who pay a lot of attention to drug use clamor to get a look at a study that largely escapes parents across the United States.

Called Monitoring the Future, it is a nationally representative survey of American students that examines their substance use and attitudes toward alcohol and other drugs.[1] The voluminous report is funded by the National Institute on Drug Abuse and produced by researchers at the University of Michigan. It is based on the anonymously self-reported surveys of about forty-five thousand middle school and high school students on about four hundred campuses. The survey began in 1975 by asking questions of high school seniors. In 1991, it expanded to include eighth- and tenth-graders. Researchers even send yearly follow-up questionnaires to a sample of every graduating class to glean information from students for several years after their initial participation.

AMONG THE THINGS WE LEARNED IN 2013

- Alcohol is the substance teenagers use more than any other. Nearly 69 percent of high school seniors, or seven out of every ten, said they had tried alcohol in an amount of "more than just a few sips." More than half of seniors, 52 percent, reported they had been drunk at least once in their lifetime. Meanwhile, back in middle school, about three out of ten, or 28 percent, of students said they had used alcohol by eighth grade—and 12 percent said they'd been drunk at least once. Among college students surveyed, 35 percent said they had consumed at least five alcoholic drinks in a row in the previous two weeks. Researchers noted what they called "particularly worrisome" rates of "extreme binge drinking." Averaged across 2005 to 2013, one in eight college students, or 13 percent, reported consuming ten or more drinks in a row in the two weeks leading up to the survey—and one in twenty, or 5 percent, reported having fifteen or more drinks in that period.[2]

- About 38 percent of high school seniors had used tobacco at least once in their lifetime. While that level is still concerning, it is part of a longtime downward trend. The larger context of tobacco use rates tells an interesting story about how social acceptance of substances influences use. The proportion of high school seniors who have ever tried cigarettes has fallen dramatically from peak levels reached between the start of 1996 and the end of 1997, when 70 percent of twelfth-graders reported they'd tried tobacco. Researchers attribute the sharp drop in use to several factors, including overall increases in students' perceptions about the risks of using, disapproval of smoking, a drop in cigarette advertising, and a spike in antismoking messaging that reached children. Researchers also noted higher tobacco costs: "Cigarette prices rose appreciably in the late 1990s and early 2000s as cigarette companies tried to cover the costs of the tobacco settlement, and as many states increased excise taxes on cigarettes," they wrote. "More recently, there was a significant increase in the federal tobacco tax passed in 2009, which may have contributed to the continuation of the decline in use since then."[3]

- Forty-five percent of high school seniors had used marijuana, the most popular illicit drug—and of that group, 6.5 percent reported using every day, up from the 2.3 percent of students who reported daily use in 1993. The rates of past-month use reported by eighth-, tenth-, and twelfth-graders increased over the previous year 1.2 percent, 4.2 percent, and 3.3 percent respectively. Daily or near-daily marijuana use—defined as twenty or more occasions of use in the previous thirty days—has continued to climb among college students too. The rate has increased from 3.5 percent in 2007 to 5.1 percent in 2013. "This is the highest rate of daily use observed among college students since 1981—a third of a century ago," said Lloyd Johnston, the study's principal investigator. "In other words, one in every 20 college students was smoking pot on a daily or near-daily basis in 2013, including one in every 11 males and one in every 34 females. To put this into a longer-term perspective, from 1990 to 1994, fewer than one in 50 college students used marijuana that frequently."[4]

- Nonmedical use of the amphetamine Adderall, a prescription drug commonly used to treat attention deficit hyperactivity disorder, ranks second among the illicit drugs college students use—reportedly to stay awake and concentrate while studying for tests. In 2013, 11 percent of college students, or one in nine, reported Adderall use without medical supervision in the previous twelve months.[5] This finding is significant because Adderall can have very serious adverse effects, and even cause death, if used improperly.

- Female college students are much less likely to use drugs than their male counterparts. For example, 33 percent of young women reported marijuana use in the past year, compared to 40 percent of young men. Similarly, 24 percent of males reported illicit drug use other than marijuana, compared to 16 percent of females. Among daily or near-daily marijuana users reporting twenty or more uses of marijuana in the previous thirty days, 9 percent were male, and 3 percent were female.[6]

- Young adults one to four years out of high school who either didn't make it to college or are enrolled part-time are twice as likely as their full-time college-student peers to be daily marijuana users. They also report past-year use rates of especially dangerous drugs—including crack cocaine, crystal methamphetamine, heroin, and other narcotics—at rates roughly two to three times higher than those found among college students. The same is true of daily cigarette smoking, which they also reported at a rate roughly three times higher than college students.[7]

If so many teens are using these substances, what's the big deal, right? Isn't it normal to experiment like this? After all, teens will be teens—and a lot of parents had their own flings with smokes and drinks, so shouldn't we just chill out and let our kids navigate the world of substances in much the same way we were expected to?

That sounds like a plan—if you take your cues from industries selling addictive substances and are good with remaining in twentieth-century mindsets and approaches to drug prevention and treatment.

Science of only the last decade is sounding serious alarms about adolescent drug use. In just the last five years, researchers have discovered more about adolescent brain development than the world ever has known. Unfortunately, the gap between what reputable science knows about adolescent substance use and what the general public believes about it has never been wider.

People profiting and otherwise benefiting from the sale of addictive substances want to keep it that way. The alcohol and tobacco industries maintain legions of lobbyists to influence public drug policies and spend billions of dollars on media each year to influence public opinion. Now, the marijuana industry is on the rise—fueled largely by legislative and popular votes that opened the doors to more mountains of misinformation.

"People are voting without the knowledge," Dr. Nora Volkow, director of the National Institute on Drug Abuse, told a ballroom packed with hundreds of drug-prevention experts, treatment providers, and concerned parents in February 2014. "And we have to counter investments of individuals wanting to change the culture and promote beliefs that marijuana is a safe drug."[8]

Yet it's very hard to hear addiction scientists and world-recognized substance treatment experts like Dr. Volkow and all the peer-reviewed research studies published in prominent medical journals over the din of billion-dollar advertising and public relations campaigns launched by companies deriving most of their profits from addiction. They want us either stuck in outdated mindsets or embracing their latest clever—and often insidious—slogans and narratives because they fear what would happen if more of us understood brain development science of the twenty-first century and challenged ourselves and our communities to rethink public policies and social norms surrounding drug and alcohol use.

The latest science boils down to this: adolescent substance use is a very big deal—and a bigger deal than researchers previously thought. Parents do not have to accept it, and when they reject the messages of popular culture that so often ensnare youth, they should know they've got reputable science on their side.

So let's take a look at the young people we're trying to protect—and cover some basic biology about them.

THE ADOLESCENT BRAIN

Anyone who has made it through adolescence knows this is a time of profoundly important development. The body changes rapidly—and the brain is obviously part of the body. Let's focus there, because it's the body's command center.

Science has known for many years that the brain achieves its maximum size and weight at about age six. What researchers didn't know until the start of the twenty-first century is that the brain fully matures around the age of twenty-four. Today—and indefinitely—scientists are studying the brain's development and functionality to understand its journey from conception through maturity.

What we know already about that journey is that during adolescence, the brain changes rapidly and works hard to become more efficient. The brain wraps its nerve cells in fat, called myelin, which is like insulation that helps its electrical signals travel more productively. During adolescence, the brain also rids itself of connections it no longer needs or uses, and this pruning also contributes to the brain's efficiency.[9]

Because the adolescent brain is under this serious construction, it is especially sensitive to harm. Think of it in the same way you would a fetus, which can be sensitive to the medications its mother takes. That's why doctors strongly recommend that women who are pregnant, or even thinking about becoming pregnant, limit their medications. The doctors do not wait for a double-blind, placebo-controlled study to show a particular medication is unsafe before they urge caution. Instead they expect medications to prove themselves safe before they recommend them to women who are pregnant. Why? Because they recognize that even relatively small outside environmental factors can have profound effects on the baby growing in the womb.

We should view the developing adolescent brain with similar care and caution—especially within the context of substance use, because it is especially vulnerable to addiction.

Here's a quick run of a few numbers showing how easily teens become addicted to substances:

- The odds of lifetime alcohol dependence decrease by 14 percent for each year the onset of alcohol use is delayed.[10]
- Similarly, the odds of lifetime drug dependence decrease by 4 percent for each year drug use is delayed.[11]
- To put it another way, 40 percent of people who start drinking by age fourteen develop alcohol dependence, compared to 10 percent of those who start drinking at age twenty.[12]
- Twenty-seven percent of those trying a drug, such as cocaine, marijuana, or prescription pain medication (without a prescription), by age fourteen develop dependence on the drug, compared to 11 percent for those waiting until age twenty.[13]

The reason adolescents become addicted more easily than adults has to do with brain development. The brain develops from the bottom up and from the back forward.[14] This sequence means the reward circuit, which includes the nucleus acumbens as shown in figure 1.1, is located near the bottom of the brain matures in early adolescence—which is a very big deal because the brain reward circuit is the channel through which everyone experiences rewards and pleasures. When it matures, adolescents experience rewards and pleasures as adults.

Biologically, this also means kids are off to the races with fully functioning gas pedals and no brakes. That's because the prefrontal cortex, which helps us plan, organize, and consider consequences, is located in the upper, front part of the brain—and won't be developed until someone reaches his or her midtwenties. The amygdala, which helps process emotions, also isn't fully developed, so adolescents may not read and understand body language and social cues as well as they will later. The bottom line: adolescents simply don't control their emotions, reason, or think ahead as well as they will when their brains are fully formed.

This imbalance in the way the brain develops could be a good thing if it encourages teens and young adults to take some risks—such as leaving home and finding a mate—but it presents big challenges that should underscore for all of us that adolescents are not merely little adults.

Adolescence is an especially risky time in life because youth respond favorably to pleasure and to the thrills of various chases, but they don't have the mature ability to control their impulses when seeking them. This helps explain why young people will sometimes do dangerous and

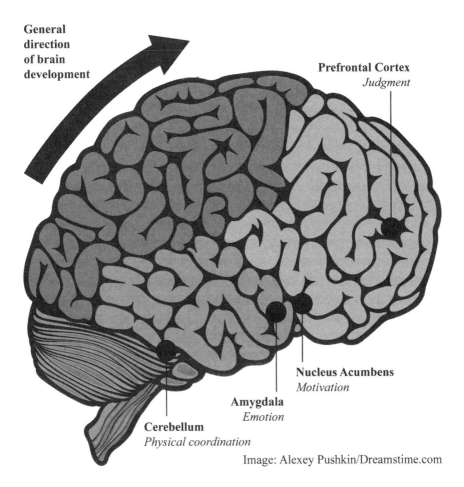

General
direction
of brain
development

Prefrontal Cortex
Judgment

Nucleus Acumbens
Motivation

Amygdala
Emotion

Cerebellum
Physical coordination

Image: Alexey Pushkin/Dreamstime.com

Figure 1.1.   Schematic of the brain.

unwise things, such as driving a parent's car without a license, stealing a street sign, or sending nude images of themselves via a mobile device without thinking through the potential consequences. It also explains why they experience pleasure with drugs and alcohol—but don't have the full ability to resist the urge to use them.

All this science is important to remember when approaching your teen to discuss anything—but especially when you want to talk with him or her about drug use and addiction. Adolescents may look like adults physically, but they do not think as adults.

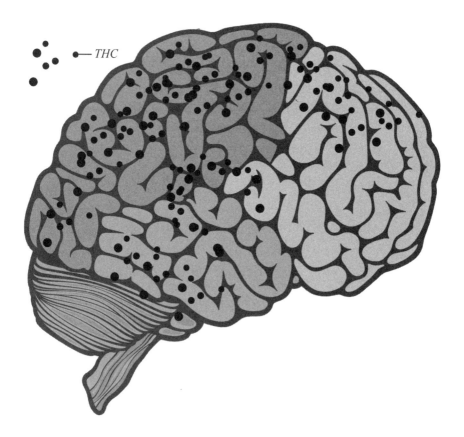

— THC

Figure 1.2.   Places in the brain where marijuana's principal ingredient, THC, is active.

WHAT THE LATEST SCIENCE TELLS US

The only way to prove definitively that adolescent exposure to drugs and alcohol causes brain damage is through a randomized, placebo-controlled study. Such a study would randomize half of the adolescents signed up to a potential neurotoxin, such as alcohol, and half to placebo—and then researchers would examine results to see who gets brain damage over time.

Want to enroll your child in this experiment? No? Good. Such a research study would be highly unethical.

This leaves us to rely on a preponderance of animal and human research showing the damaging effects of substance exposure. We also must rely on common sense—and we should certainly rely on lessons learned from our experience with the tobacco industry, which has spent millions of dollars on misinformation campaigns to challenge connections between smoking and cancer and the harmful effects of secondhand smoke. All the while, the companies squarely aimed their messages at kids—as was discovered among their internal memos, made public during the American tobacco settlements of the 1990s. Many of the tobacco companies' stated observations about the initiation of adolescent use—and even the grooming of what were referred to as "presmokers"—could just as easily be applied to other addictive substances.

Consider these statements, which informed tobacco companies' advertising and business development efforts for many years:

From Philip Morris in 1969: "Smoking a cigarette for the beginner is a symbolic act. . . . 'I am no longer my mother's child, I'm tough, I am an adventurer, I'm not square.' . . . As the force from the psychological symbolism subsides, the pharmacological effect takes over to sustain the habit."[15]

From R. J. Reynolds in 1973: "Realistically, if our Company is to survive and prosper, over the long term we must get our share of the youth market."[16]

From Brown & Williamson in 1980: "The studies reported on youngsters' motivation for starting, their brand preferences, etc., as well as the starting behavior of children as young as 5 years old. . . . The studies examined examination [sic] of young smokers' attitudes towards 'addiction,' and contain multiple references to how very young smokers at first believe they cannot become addicted, only to later discover, to their regret, that they are."[17]

From Lorillard in 1970: "We're adults. You've got a group of talented kids. Hence this letter. We have been asked by our client to come up with a package design . . . a design that is attractive to kids. . . . While this cigarette is geared to the youth market, no attempt (obvious) can be made to encourage persons under twenty-one to smoke. The package design should be geared to attract the youthful eye . . . not the ever-watchful eye of the Federal Government."[18]

Big Tobacco's strategies raised just enough doubt to delay for seven decades public health approaches and policy changes that eventually reduced smoking rates and secondhand exposure. Unfortunately, our country's delay in seeing through the industry's smoke and mirrors contributed to hundreds of thousands of deaths. We cannot afford to make similar mistakes again.

Current science has confirmed what anyone selling an addictive substance also knows: youth are especially vulnerable to addiction, and they're the golden key to building a lifelong customer base. Many studies in animals and humans show adolescent exposure to addictive substances predicts various brain changes in adulthood—relatively new science that should prompt us to ask hard questions about adult attitudes and social norms related to substances.

Let's take a look at some of the latest research focused on adolescent use of the "big three"—tobacco, alcohol, and marijuana, which teens are most likely to use.

Tobacco

In animals, adolescent exposure to nicotine causes permanent deficits in attention and impulsivity.[19] While we cannot ethically conduct these studies in humans, human research is consistent with studies performed in animals.[20] Human studies also show that adolescent exposure to tobacco predicts subsequent symptoms of depression in girls.[21]

"Design changes and chemical additives introduced by tobacco companies in recent decades have made cigarettes more addictive, more attractive to kids and even more deadly," the Campaign for Tobacco-Free Kids, a nonprofit organization that claims to accept no government or tobacco-industry funding, stated in its June 2014 report, "Designed for Addiction."[22] The report, which is based on an extensive review of scientific research and tobacco-industry documents, identifies several ways that the engineering of today's cigarettes plays on the developing brain:

- Increased nicotine. "Tobacco companies precisely control the delivery and amount of nicotine to create and sustain addiction."
- New and increased additives in tobacco. "Tobacco companies know that 90 percent of adult smokers start at or before age 18 and that smoking is unpleasant for new smokers, so they use chemical additives to make tobacco smoke smoother, less harsh and more appealing to the young, novice smoker."

- New designs aimed at getting users to inhale more "vigorously." "Cigarettes with ventilated filters were introduced by tobacco companies because they produced lower levels of tar and nicotine in machine tests and were marketed as less hazardous. However, the evidence now shows that these cigarettes did not reduce health risks and likely increased smokers' risk of lung cancer"—an assertion consistent with the U.S. Surgeon General's 2014 report.[23]

Alcohol

Similarly, alcohol is toxic to brain development. For example, mice and rats exposed to a binge-drinking paradigm during adolescence show deficits in certain types of learning, increased risk taking, and increased vulnerability to alcohol dependence as adults.[24,25] The exposed animals compared to those not exposed to alcohol during adolescence also show changes in important brain structures having to do with behavior, coordination, learning, and memory.

Human studies show similar findings. For example, adolescents with a history of drinking five or more drinks in a row have a greater reduction in the volume of at least 15 different brain structures at three-year follow-up than their peers without a binge-drinking history.[26] The same study showed that adolescent binge drinking is associated with changes in the connections between various brain structures, and these changes, in turn, are associated with a general reduction in language and spatial thinking abilities.[27]

Marijuana

Far too many parents describe it as "just pot" until they experience firsthand a child addicted to the drug. Marijuana addiction is the top reason youth in the United States are admitted for substance abuse treatment.

It's important to focus on marijuana because of its recent rise in popularity and the common myth that it is relatively harmless compared to alcohol and tobacco. On the contrary, recent research shows that marijuana is more harmful to brain development than previously thought.

In fact, tetrahydrocannabinol, or THC, the active ingredient in marijuana that produces the euphoric high users experience, binds to the very receptor, called the cannabinoid 1 receptor, that helps control adolescent brain development.[28] As shown in figure 1.2, THC is active in many parts of the brain.

Here are some of the latest findings about marijuana use during adolescence:

- Animal studies show it causes deficits in attention, decreased motivation, decreased short-term memory, and more anxious social interactions in adults.[29] These brain changes are permanent and associated with notable damage to parts of the brain such as the hippocampus, an important structure for learning and memory.[30]
- In humans, heavy exposure to marijuana starting in adolescence predicts up to an eight-point drop in IQ from age thirteen to age thirty-eight.[31] The study findings suggest the drop in IQ is permanent and dose-dependent—meaning the more marijuana used, the greater the drop in IQ. The study found that only first use of marijuana during adolescence, not onset during adulthood, predicted the drop in IQ. The study controlled for other co-occurring psychiatric disorders, substance use, school achievement, and socioeconomic status.[32]
- In humans, adolescent exposure to marijuana predicts a doubling in the risk of psychosis in adulthood. Psychosis includes hearing and seeing things that aren't there. It also includes delusions, or fixed, false beliefs not shared by the larger community. The increased risk for psychosis starts with a single exposure to marijuana, and the risk is dose-dependent—meaning the more marijuana someone uses, the greater his or her risk of psychosis. This finding first was reported in 1988 and has been replicated at least five times. These studies have controlled for dozens of possible, confounding variables,[33] and all yield similar results.
- Adolescent exposure to marijuana predicts a doubling in the odds of having an anxiety disorder in adulthood.[34]
- Adolescents who use marijuana are at least twice as likely to go on to use other substances, compared to those who do not use the drug.[35]

- Recent research shows that marijuana use is associated with significant changes in brain structure. For example, people with a past history of cannabis use disorder have significant differences in the hippocampus, an important structure for learning and memory, compared to controls.[36]
- Another study shows that young adults who use marijuana casually (one to two times a week) have differences in brain structures having to do with emotion and brain reward compared with controls.[37]

A Word about the "Gateway"

There is much debate about the "gateway hypothesis"—meaning the likelihood that people who use one drug move on to other drugs. Because it is poorly understood and the source of much contention, it is important to examine this aspect of drug use and addiction.

Simply put, not everyone who uses an addictive substance goes on to use another more potent one—but a percentage of people do. Take a hard look at their medical histories, and you are likely to find they first reached for an addictive drug during adolescence. Take marijuana, for example. Of the approximately 2.4 million people in the United States who try the drug for the first time each year, almost 60 percent are under the age of eighteen, according to the National Survey on Drug Use and Health.

Multiple studies conducted around the world have documented the gateway pattern of substance use, and because the pattern is so clearly observed, there is little debate about it among reputable scientists. It typically starts with alcohol and tobacco, progresses to marijuana, and moves on to other substances. The risk starts with a single use, and it is increased with early onset of use and regular use.[38] For example, multiple studies from across the globe and involving tens of thousands of research participants show teens who use marijuana are 22 to 1,479 times more likely to go on to use other substances than teens who don't, depending on the country and the study.[39] Similarly, adolescents who use alcohol or tobacco are 1.7 to 225 times more likely to use other substances than those who don't, again depending on the country and the study.[40]

Popular musician Lady Gaga came up with another way to describe the "gateway" scientists study when she spoke with a radio personality about her marijuana addiction in 2013.[41] "I have been addicted to various things since I was young, and most heavily over the past seven years. . . . A friend gave me this term: I 'lily pad' from substance to substance because I get to a point where I can't go any further with one substance, so I have to move to another. Yes, it can be [frightening]."

So the debate among scientists isn't about whether the gateway pattern is observed or whether youth who use alcohol, tobacco, or marijuana are more likely to progress to other substance use. It is, and they are. Rather, the debate is focused on why the pattern is observed and why young people move from one substance to the next.

Studies of twins, which can control for differences in environment and genetic influences, show the reason for the gateway progression is likely a combination of the following three explanations:[42]

1. Gateway substances may cause the brain to respond more favorably to other substances later in life. This explanation is supported by animal studies showing adolescent exposure to alcohol, marijuana, or nicotine causes a more favorable response to other substances in adulthood. For example, mice exposed to nicotine during adolescence (days 28 to 56 of life for mice), compared to those who are not exposed to nicotine during adolescence, self-administer more cocaine as adults.[43] Similarly, rats exposed to marijuana during adolescence, compared to those not exposed, self-administer more heroin as adults.[44]

2. Teens who know where to get alcohol, tobacco, and marijuana also know where to get other substances and also have friends who use other substances. This explanation is social, not biological. Teens who know where to obtain one substance may be more likely to have friends and contacts who can also provide others. For example, one study of twelve- to twenty-five-year-olds showed that 13 percent of youth who had never used alcohol, tobacco, or marijuana reported ever having an opportunity to use cocaine. Of students reporting they'd used alcohol and tobacco, 26 percent said they'd had the chance to use cocaine. Of those who reported marijuana use, 51 percent reported they'd had the opportunity. And what about youth who reported ever using all

three drugs? A full 75 percent of them reported they'd had an opportunity to use cocaine.[45]

3. There may be an underlying genetic trait that causes teens to have multiple risky behaviors, including substance use and unprotected sex. This explanation is supported by findings showing that youth who use substances are more likely to engage in potentially harmful behaviors, such as aggression, early sexual involvement, and school dropout. For example, about half of teens in substance treatment have co-occurring conduct disorder, which consists of a variety of symptoms, such as fighting, stealing, and truancy.[46, 47]

One final note about "gateway substances," which people often call "soft" drugs: they are, in and of themselves, harmful even if their use does not progress to use of "hard drugs." For example, cigarette smoking is the leading cause of preventable death in the United States, and alcohol use is the third leading cause.[48] These are supposedly soft drugs—and yet the death and destruction they cause is undeniable. So the distinction between "soft" and "hard" drugs isn't based on actual science—and adolescent use of gateway substances is, in and of itself, an important problem. It's not "just beer" or "just pot" or "just a cigarette," especially when it comes to kids.

ADOLESCENTS DON'T NEED MORE SOCIAL PROBLEMS

Even if teen substance use doesn't appear to affect brain development or cause important biological effects, it predicts many social problems:

- Academic achievement is an important predictor of many life outcomes, including overall quality of life.[49] Youth who use marijuana by the age of fifteen are about four times less likely to complete high school, compared to students who do not use marijuana or who wait until they are at least eighteen years old to try the drug.[50] In September 2014, researchers at Australia's National Drug and Alcohol Research Center also reported in the prestigious medical journal *Lancet Psychiatry* that when compared with nonusers, daily users of cannabis before age seventeen are more

than 60 percent less likely to complete high school or obtain a college degree, seven times more likely to attempt suicide, and eight times more likely to use other illicit drugs.[51]
- Teen substance use is associated with car crashes, the leading cause of death for fifteen- to twenty-year-olds.
- Teens who use drugs are more likely to engage in high-risk sex, including unprotected sex with multiple partners.[52,53,54]

If there's good news to be found in this chapter, it's this: parents who are informed about the potential harms of drug use can do much to influence their child's decision making. We'll learn much more about that in upcoming chapters.

THE TREATMENT PROVIDER'S PERSPECTIVE

"The science is not usually the place to start a conversation with most kids, who pretty much think only in terms of social problems," said Amy Weiland,[55] who, along with her husband, Mike, directs the Missouri-based Crossroads Program that has helped hundreds of young people achieve sobriety over the last two decades.

"But this brain stuff is really important for parents to know—especially parents today—because the risks and the problems are very real. When you know the science, you'll start to think a lot differently about how to approach drug use with your kids. Our conventional wisdom hasn't always been so wise.

"The reality of doing drugs is now very different from the realities parents faced when they were young. A lot of times, moms and dads try to take their own personal experiences from high school or college and relate them to their children. Nine times out of ten, parents who have a history of their own drug use say to me, 'They're like I was, and I was able to go through it with no problem. I'm successful.'

"When parents do this, they'll miss so much, because that's just not how things work today. Our culture is so different, and our media are nonstop and more interconnected than ever. There are social pressures on kids that their parents never dreamed about. Add to all of this the higher potency of pot, the lowered perception of harm with marijuana, and the constant advertising of alcohol just about everywhere, and that's the adolescent drug scene today. It's intense."

Insight from the World of Recovery

"Remembering how I was when I was in middle school and high school? If you'd told me about how using drugs would harm my brain, I wouldn't have cared," said Raymond N., who is in his early twenties and in substance recovery in Saint Louis, Missouri. "A lot of the stuff we learned in classes and health programs and other initiatives was in one ear and out the other. But today? The brain science is interesting, and I can understand it. Because of my experiences, I know now that we have to find better ways to teach these concepts."

DISCUSSION QUESTIONS

- *How would you summarize adolescent brain development? What are the consequences of adolescent drug use that are most relevant for you?*
- *How does adolescent brain development as outlined in this chapter affect your understanding about addiction and people who suffer from it?*
- *How does your understanding of adolescent brain development affect your views of social norms surrounding use of drugs and alcohol?*

2

PARENTS' TOOLS FOR PLANNING, COMMUNICATING, AND MONITORING

Preventing and addressing drug use and abuse are not a spectator sport. They require direct conversation and engagement—and there is no clock to say time's up.

While it's important to speak with the head, it's just as important—perhaps even more so—to speak from the heart. Education about a drug's effects on the body and communities is vital, but it's only half of the equation to communicate to young people. The other half focuses on helping children and teens understand that drug use is unacceptable because they're loved, valued, and uniquely gifted to make positive differences in the world. The ideal approach is one that communicates, "People in the know just say no because they've found healthier and better ways to feel great about who they are and how they can help others. Their highs are the real thing."

As if this balance isn't tough enough to navigate, parents must walk another fine line—one that differentiates between drug experimentation and substance use disorder. Calling in teams of addiction treatment providers before they're necessary could cause a lot of relational damage. On the other hand, denying a substance problem often has far worse consequences.

"One of the first things parents who come to me always ask is, 'Why did my kid do this?'" said Father John Bonavitacola,[1] pastor of Our Lady of Mount Carmel Parish in Tempe, Arizona, where he helps lead a Catholic school for students in prekindergarten through grade 8 and a program called Full Circle for teens struggling with substance abuse and addiction. Father Bonavitacola is a recovering alcoholic whose personal experience has helped hundreds of families navigate the hurts and harms of addiction and rebuild relationships in recovery.

"You know what the answer usually is?" he continued. "The kids say, 'Because it was fun, Mom and Dad. All of the kids were doing it, and it was fun. End of story. No need to fish for a deep psychological problem.'

"So we don't go into deep psychological issues, but we do address the problem of the child associating getting high with something fun," Father Bonavitacola said. "We help parents make it clear the behavior has to stop and why it has to stop, and we help them explain the consequences that will follow if it doesn't."

Then there are the parents Amy and Mike Weiland,[2] the substance treatment providers in Missouri, often see.

"They tell us all about how their kid is 'just experimenting' or 'just dabbling,'" Mike Weiland said. "When we ask more questions, we learn this has been going on for months or even years. What a great way to deny what's really happening."

Added Amy Weiland: "Very rarely does a kid get caught the first time he or she uses. If you find a drug, it's a problem—and no, your child is never, ever holding it for a friend. The definition of an experiment is that you do something once, then you do it a second time to confirm the result. If you do it a third time, it's because you know the outcome, and you think it's awesome—and now you're no longer experimenting."

Good parents—very loving, attentive, consistent, and otherwise caring parents—often have no idea their child has a substance problem until it's so obvious the only reasonable thing to do is find professional help. They've seemingly done everything well. They've spent time with their children. They've encouraged social activities. They've helped with homework. They've cheered at every sporting event. They've listened carefully and have empathized when needed.

And still their child picked up a drug—or two or three drugs—and couldn't put them down.

This scenario, which regularly plays out in addiction treatment specialists' offices, should tell us at least three things:

- Parents are not necessarily to blame for their child's substance problems—and "good parenting" isn't all that's required to discourage adolescent drug use.
- Societal pressure, particularly when exerted by peers and influential adults and amplified by media and commercialization, is a powerful force.
- Parents must vigilantly—and unapologetically—be on the lookout for possible drug and alcohol use and abuse by their children.

Before we unpack what that vigilance should look like, it's important to know about the three main drivers of substance abuse and addiction in any community. Drug policy makers and scientists pay careful attention to these things, and parents would also benefit from understanding them. Continually surveying our homes and our children's social circles through a lens trained on these three things could help prevent drug use and catch problems early:

- **Access to substances:** The more easily a substance is had, the more likely it is to be used. This principle applies to individual homes and larger communities. Usually a teen's first taste of tobacco or alcohol happens when they access their parents' stash. So think seriously about where you keep drugs in your home.[3]
- **Social acceptance of substance use:** The more socially accepted substance use is—whether that's communicated by billboards and storefronts along a highway or by teens at a Friday night party, or by parents who use drugs and alcohol in front of their children—the more likely substances are to be used. [4]
- **Perceived risk of harm:** When someone perceives a substance might harm them and is concerned about that harm, they are less likely to use that substance. Researchers carefully study the rates of these perceptions in adolescents and communities because they predict future drug use by about two years.[5]

When access to substances and social acceptance of substance use increase, and the perceived risk of harm decreases, the rates of substance use and addiction rise. This is true for entire nations—and it is also true for your household and the households where your teen likes to spend time.

Knowing the three main drivers of substance use can help us evaluate the healthiness of an adolescent's various social environments and also inform our efforts to help the youth we care about navigate the inevitable times when they'll feel pressured to try a substance.

Which brings us back to parental vigilance. The especially good news for parents is that they have evidence-based tools to work with and a great deal of influence over their kids. There are many ways to discuss substances with your children and to monitor their lives for signs of a problem—and all tend to be built on this foundation:

HAVING A POSITIVE RELATIONSHIP WITH YOUR CHILD

Of everything parents can do, this is the most important. Children grow up to incorporate the positive values of their parents by having a warm relationship with them. This doesn't mean parents shouldn't enforce rules or that they should act as their child's buddy (after all, friends don't send friends to college). However, it does mean parents should spend time with their children, regularly doing pleasant things together. Perhaps that's cooking, camping, playing cards or sports, heading off to the museum, shopping, or watching a movie and discussing it over dinner. The idea is to pay attention to what interests your teen—and then follow up with conversation and activity focused there.

When in doubt about your child's feelings, beliefs, attitudes, or actions, always come back to this point and consider it your grounding force.

MAINTAINING COMMUNICATION

If two people spend time together and are in a loving and respectful relationship, they obviously communicate. There are a few key ways to help ensure healthy contact:

- **Talk about what interests your teen.** Let them tell you about their musical interests, their frustration with math, or the interpersonal high school drama of the day. Go where they want to take the conversation. Don't answer the phone. Don't check e-mail. Don't watch television. Don't let yourself get otherwise distracted. Do make eye contact and give them your undivided attention.

- **Make small talk.** Big things are made of small things—so small talk about the weather or the kind of cereal your teen likes is actually important. These friendly and inquisitive exchanges communicate you're paying attention to the details and that you care. Eventually they add up—and they often provide the opening your teen is looking for to discuss something of seemingly greater importance.
- **Be inquisitive, not accusatory.** No one likes being pounced on or interrogated. Accusation, speculation, and assumption quickly lead to breakdowns in communication and trust. When you ask a question, ask because you are curious, not because you are trying to make a point. If you need to make a point, then make your point directly, but first try to understand where your teen is coming from.
- **Maintain an always-open-door policy.** Remind your child early and often that you'll always try to be available when they want you to listen to them.

When it comes to substances, there is no one, big "drug talk." Instead, communicating expectations and the reasons for those expectations takes a series of conversations over time—ideally starting at a very young age. It's important to adjust your approach as a child matures. Parents of a six-year-old should communicate in fairly concrete terms—for example, "Drugs are bad." However, far more subtle conversations tend to be more effective with teens. Every so often, parents should ask:

- "What do you think about alcohol, marijuana, tobacco, and other drugs?"
- "What do your friends think about drugs and alcohol?"
- "Are any of your friends using drugs or alcohol?"
- "Have you ever noticed an older kid or adult who seems to have a problem with drugs or alcohol?"
- "What do you think that ad wants you to believe about that drug? Is that reality?"
- "Have you used drugs or alcohol?"

"Don't count on getting an honest answer to that last question," Father Bonavitacola said. "But ask it, because that will force your child to face the truth even if he or she doesn't come clean to you."

Your conversations about drug use should also be:

- **Timely.** Ideally, parents will raise the subject of drug use in the moments it comes up. Maybe that's when you're listening to a newscast, walking past a storefront, or attending a public event. Perhaps it's when you know your child is studying about drug use in a class, or when you know the topic is raised during an after-school youth group.
- **Personally relevant to your child.** Perhaps he or she already has noticed classmates or family members who have substance problems. There are lessons to learn from those relationships.
- **Direct and clear.** It's common for young people in substance treatment to relay that they don't think one or both parents care about their drug use. Parents should explicitly state their disapproval of substance abuse and their expectations of their child—and they should use a united front to do so. That way, their teen won't be able to say something along the lines of, "My mom doesn't want me to smoke weed, but my dad doesn't care if I do."
- **Open.** A my-way-or-the-highway approach to teens often backfires. Parents should be open to questions and some challenges. Rarely does anyone have all the answers, and there's nothing wrong with admitting that. If anything, differing points of view are an opportunity for parents to work with their children to learn how and why drug use can be harmful. Together they also can learn more about what are and are not reliable and trustworthy sources of information.
- **Loving.** These are times to reiterate your love for your child. "I love you, and I want to help you reach your full potential and be the best at whatever you choose to do. I also don't want you to risk the problems—sometimes really serious problems that are not easily fixed—that can go along with drug use. That is why I hope you'll maintain a clear mind and take care of your brain."

"Okay, so, Mom and Dad, what did you do when you were a teenager? Have you ever used drugs?"

Cue the horror soundtrack here. This is the part of the conversation so many parents dread. While good parents can disagree about when and how much to share with their children about their own drug history, every discussion should flow from honesty—especially because addiction is a disease fraught with manipulation and lying. Youth really do want their parents to speak truthfully and transparently.

However, here are some general guidelines to consider:

- **Children twelve to sixteen:** Avoid discussing your past drug use. Keep the conversation focused as much as possible on the harms of using drugs and the benefits of not using them. When asked directly, parents might say that yes, they've tried alcohol, tobacco, or marijuana, but they should avoid sharing any other details about their experiences because there is too much risk that this information will be misunderstood and misused by children in this age range. Parents should also express regret for their drug use.
- **Children seventeen and older:** Parents should use their best judgment about what to share—but they should take great care not to glorify their drug experiences or minimize the potential or real harms of their drug use. This might be the time to discuss in more detail how alcohol or drug abuse has negatively affected people in your family or social circles. The message to impart is that drug use is not what you want for your teen.

"I see it all the time," said Josh Azevedo,[6] a licensed independent substance abuse counselor who directs The Pathway Program in Phoenix, Arizona, and has been in substance recovery for more than two decades. "A lot of parents glorify their drug use. They tell these stories about high school and college and the time they did this or that, and they make it all sound like it was so much fun, the greatest time ever, and something their kids will have a chance to experience. Then, when I ask, I find out that the parents maybe got drunk four times total in their lives and never had a problem—but now they've got a kid in treatment who's saying, 'I wanted to create those good times for myself.'"

When speaking with youth about drug use, it's obviously important to cover the risks and harms—but it's just as important to explain that a lot of people use drugs because they love the way they make them feel. We shouldn't shy away from discussing with older teens the euphoria substance users experience. They're having a great time while under the influence. They believe they're the life of a party, bonding with friends, expanding their minds, enhancing their creativity, on top of the world, completely care-free.

It can be a real love affair—which is why a typical lament of people in substance treatment goes like this: "Everyone told me about DUI, flunking out of school, losing a job, and sprouting a third eye, but those things never happened. What I wish someone had told me is how much I would fall in love with drugs—and with everything that comes with them. I wish someone had told me that I would love a drug so much I would never want to stop using it, and that it would take over. It would become the love of my life, and I would let a lot of people and important things go to have it instead."

MONITORING FRIENDS AND WHEREABOUTS

In general, parents should know at all times where their teen is and whom they're with. This becomes more difficult as children age, but that doesn't make it any less important. It is a parent's right and responsibility to supervise and monitor—and appropriate supervision works. It reduces problem behavior and helps youth grow up healthy and strong.

At the same time, it is very important for supervision and monitoring to be age-appropriate and to reflect the trust a teen has earned. An eighteen-year-old who hasn't had any problems will need less monitoring than another person the same age who is obviously struggling.

The people with whom we most closely associate and the places where we spend our time profoundly shape our own beliefs and behaviors. So if we wish to prevent substance use—whether that's initial use or a relapse—our aim should be to ensure youth are surrounded by healthy environments where they experience the joy of "earned" or "natural" highs that come from things like academic achievement, a sports championship, community service, or just hanging out with a friend who also likes to paint or build software.

To do the mission-critically important job of monitoring friends and whereabouts, parents need a plan and the commitment to stick to it. They should:

- Emphasize that they're on their child's team. This effort should reinforce a parent's desire to maintain the positive relationship detailed earlier in this chapter. Teamwork doesn't mean you always agree or that you even necessarily like each other in every situation. Teamwork also doesn't mean parents don't parent: they are, instead, responsible for helping their child understand how to build an even bigger team that includes their child's friends, other parents, educators, coaches, family members, and anyone else who shares in the common goal of avoiding the harms that can come from substance use. Showing young people how to build effective teams will serve them well no matter the circumstance—and for the rest of their lives.
- Work with their teen ahead of time to address difficult social situations. Indiana State Supreme Court Justice Steven H. David shares his "Rules for Parenting" with hundreds of Hoosier parents each year. He emphasizes the rewards that come from this aspect of sincere parent-child teamwork: "Make it clear to your child that he or she may use you as the bad guy anytime. If they aren't able to make a decision on their own, tell them to use you and abuse you. In other words, if they are at a party, and the drugs arrive, and they are offered and encouraged, you will have already talked with them about how they could handle that situation. 'I can't do that because when I get home, I have to kiss my mom goodnight and recite the alphabet backwards.' Step up to the plate and let them squarely blame you if that helps them avoid problems. Also give them exit strategies. For example, your daughter is somewhere she should probably not be, and alcohol arrives along with a few twenty-year-olds. In that situation, she can trigger the plan you've already prearranged with her by saying, 'Oh, no. What time is it? I forgot to call my stupid parents.' Then, when she calls, and uses a key word or phrase, you'll know she means she needs you to pick her up—no matter the hour—or order her home. She gets out of the situation, and you are the bad guy—and that is okay."

- Ask their teens where they're going and with whom—and require even a brief, face-to-face meeting with everyone before they depart.
- Require teens to send a text message or call periodically to check in. Parents should take care to explain why this is important. "It's difficult for me to concentrate at work when I worry about you, so just giving me a quick heads-up every couple of hours helps me feel better. Thanks for hearing me out on that."
- Establish and enforce a curfew—and require a brief, face-to-face visit with your teen when he or she arrives home, no matter the hour. Look for signs of intoxication.
- Check with the parents of your teen's friends to make sure any event plans are consistent. After all, these people should be on your family's team too. When possible, make time to meet the parents of your child's friends—and try to learn what you can about the siblings (especially older siblings) in that family. Diversion of drugs from other parents to your child and from the older siblings of your child's friends is unfortunately too common.
- Feel free to say no to any plan that seems unwise. For this, parents must trust their intuition. Having even a hard-to-describe, inner sense that a plan is bad is good enough reason to reject it. Rarely will parents have a perfect, airtight reason to say no to their child—and that is fine. Just remember to push back calmly and without argument, because escalating conflict only makes everyone upset. Ideally, parents will offer an alternative activity or a plan that is squarely aligned with their teen's interests.

No parent can do all of this perfectly in every instance. The key is to do a good enough job at holding this ground and to avoid feeling guilty when your parenting makes your teen angry. It's imperative that parents be willing and able to handle their child's anger. They don't have to tolerate blatant disrespect, but when they're seeing the unsurprising eruption of frustration—think a haughty attitude—related to their "no," the situation is often best handled when they absorb that anger calmly and move on with their day.

LISTENING TO BEHAVIORS

Everything about your child matters, and he or she will communicate much without saying a word. So become a careful student of his or her actions. The idea is not to create excessive worry, but instead to have a chance at prevention and early intervention, which carries a much better prognosis than late intervention.

Parents are also often too quick to dismiss questionable behavior as teen angst or a phase of adolescent moodiness. Most teens make it through these tough years without much drama—so where parents think they smell smoke, there is often fire. They should trust their instincts, investigate more aggressively, and ask tough questions.

It's hard to underscore enough how important it is for parents to trust their instincts.

THE TREATMENT PROVIDER'S PERSPECTIVE

"Our program requires family involvement, and we don't take in kids who are dragged in by the ear for any reason," said Josh Azevedo. "Very rarely do we see a parent who allowed use. Instead they're the PTA parents, the parents who lead sports teams and church programs. They're actively involved and loving people—but there are places where these parents typically get into trouble, and they come down to this: they didn't trust their gut.

"A lot of times, parents notice something isn't quite right. They can't explain the feeling exactly, but they're uneasy. Instead of actually looking further, they dismiss their questions and discomfort. They tell themselves that their kid is just going through a phase and that even if they try beer a couple of times, there's no reason to say anything, because they did the same thing at that age without developing any problems.

"A lot of parents also suffer quietly because they feel they're the only ones in their set of friends or their neighborhood encouraging total abstinence, or they think they're the only ones who want to get on the same page about drugs with the parents of their child's friends—especially when the kids in question are older teens. They don't have the conversations they know they should because they're afraid of the rejection of other parents and that their kids will be rejected too. Those fears convince them to move past their better judgment and their instincts."[7]

Among the big signs to look for:

Academic and extracurricular performance. Have grades slipped? Has the soccer team or chemistry club been abandoned?

A change in friends. Have longtime childhood friends fallen out of favor? What does your child appear to have in common with her new friends?

A change in appearance. Clothing, hair, bathing routines, and other aspects of personal hygiene can be telling signs of drug use. Parents may also want to pay attention to changes in grooming, such as the heavy use of body spray, which is frequently used to cover up the smell of smoke. Sudden and prolonged use of eyedrops may be an attempt to cover up red eyes from drug use.

Noticeable and prolonged changes in mood and behavior. Drug users often seek to isolate themselves from family. They are more secretive and more interested in hanging out with their friends away from home. Dramatic personality changes are also not normal. Has your gentle, sensitive, and smart child turned into someone you don't recognize?

"In and of themselves, these things don't reveal a whole lot, but when you put them together, you'll see big changes," Father Bonavitacola said. "What you don't want to do is immediately accuse your child of using substances. You need more hard-core proof—and even when you think you have it, it's a good idea to ask a lot of questions first. 'You were always such good friends with so-and-so, and now you never talk to him. You aren't going to practice anymore. Why do you think your grades have fallen so much? How do you explain all of this? I'm confused.'

"Your questioning will give the child an opportunity to talk a little more, and it'll give you the opportunity to explain what you find acceptable—and what the consequences are if things don't change. Now at least your child knows there's a chance you'll be bringing in a third party to probe more deeply to know what, exactly, is going on."

TRACKING MEDIA AND COMMUNICATIONS

Media deserve special focus because they're so constant, pervasive—and highly influential.

For example, researchers at Washington University School of Medicine in Saint Louis examined a popular Twitter feed focused on marijuana and followed by about one million people—73 percent of whom were under the age of nineteen, and 22 percent of whom were ages twenty to twenty-four. During the eight-month study, researchers found that the account tweeted overwhelmingly pro-marijuana messages to its teen followers an average of eleven times each day.[8]

"Studies looking at media messages on traditional outlets like television, radio, billboards, and magazines have shown that media messages can influence substance use and attitudes about substance use," said Patricia A. Cavazos-Rehg, the study's principal investigator. "It's likely a young person's attitudes and behaviors may be influenced when he or she is receiving daily, ongoing messages of this sort."

So it's important to establish clear guidelines about how you expect your teen to use desktop computers, mobile phones, and any other digital networks—and enforce the rules. Pay attention to whether the musical artists and celebrities your teen follows are known for their extensive drug use or references to drugs. Pay attention to all of the organizations and causes your teen monitors on social media. Look into which news sites your child visits—because many are also awash with inaccurate information about drug use. Take the time to understand how the applications loaded on your child's mobile devices actually work.

Various applications for cell phones and computers track text messaging and e-mails and block messages from certain people. Parents should use them, and the extent to which they use them should be determined by a specific situation. For example, teens who follow the rules very well earn privacy, while teens who break the rules do not.

PARENTS WHO HAVE BEEN THERE

"We were naive about so many things, and one of the biggies was the media and culture we allowed into our home," said Jo McGuire,[9] who went to work as a compliance director for a drug-testing company in Colorado after learning about her own son's drug problems. "When my son was in middle school, he loved *That '70s Show*. My husband and I thought it was funny to show our kids that era, especially some of the clothes worn then. We didn't even give much thought to all the pot jokes because we thought our kids automatically understood the drug was bad. But later, when we learned our son was deep into the marijuana scene, we began to see how we'd allowed him to be surrounded by pro-drug messages. We'd even supplied him with the culture to a large degree. We bought him the music, the posters, the movies, and the TV shows—nearly all of which communicated that everyone smoked pot, and it was great. When my son entered treatment, I took an honest inventory of other families I knew and realized that the parents who allowed drug-glorifying media in their homes also had kids who had bought into drugs—and that the people who didn't allow those messages into their homes had fewer problems."

Insight from the World of Recovery

"There are so many big influencers of drug culture among kids that it's really hard to pinpoint a few, but the entertainment industry obviously knows what it's doing," said Raymond N., a twenty-one-year-old in substance recovery in Missouri. "References to drugs—especially pot—are so commonplace, and nothing about drugs is ever presented within the context of being a problem.

"What was always really obvious to me were food commercials. I have always known some of those fast-food restaurants are marketing straight to people who smoke pot."

CREATING A DRUG-ABUSE-FREE HOME—AND MONITORING IT

As the ones who pay all the bills and assume the responsibility of home and/or car ownership, parents have a right to know what happens under their roofs at all times, and they have the right to prohibit certain things, such as substance use.

Cue the next delicate, parental balancing act: it's the one between being caring and overbearing.

Parents will want to grant more privacy to teens who are respectful, responsible, and truthful than to teens who break clearly communicated rules—but just as with taking care not to call in third-party substance treatment providers before they're needed, parents should avoid acting out of fear. Instead their challenge is to communicate how pleased they are to help their child embrace and navigate their rapidly expanding independence.

When adolescents have consistently honored the rules and have given you no reason to suspect substance use, praise them specifically and directly. In other words, catch them being good and call them out for it. Your positive feedback could be as simple as, "Great job. I'm so proud of the good choices you're making." Parents also can follow up with privileges, such as privacy, mobile phone use, driving, and curfew extensions. Not only does this encourage more good behavior, but it communicates to your teen that you're paying attention.

However, when adolescents have not earned their privacy, diligent monitoring of friends, activities, mobile devices—and, yes, room and car searches—is reasonable. Sometimes the blow of this kind of monitoring is softened by giving advance warning of an inspection along these lines: "I'm sorry to do this, but I have reason to suspect you've been using drugs or alcohol, and that is against the rules we've discussed—and you agreed to honor. So I am going to start checking on you today and will do so regularly, sometimes when you're not here. I do not want to do this, but I am because I love you and want to protect you and everyone else in our home. Drug use potentially harms all of us."

A word about drug screens. Parents frequently ask whether they should use at-home tests to monitor their teens for substance use.

There are two common schools of thought worth considering:

- No testing until there is strong reason to believe a child has used drugs or alcohol. Routine testing when there is reason to suspect drug use.
- Testing from the start of a teen's legal driving privileges. "Drug testing can be effective if it's limited to a very small number of things, such as driving," Father Bonavitacola said. "But it really

has to be done the right way. Parents have to communicate that there are things adults do to hold themselves accountable to others in exchange for certain privileges, and that we're talking about a car that could kill people if it is misused. This is about teamwork and the acknowledgment that a great deal is at stake. Everyone has their role and responsibility, and they'll be rewarded for honoring their commitments—behavior that could be confirmed with occasional testing. It's also important for parents to explain not just what they're doing, but why they're doing it: 'Operating a car is dangerous, and I don't ever want to get a call that you've been involved in a fatal accident.'"

Drug screens can be purchased over the counter and are performed from blood, hair, saliva, or urine. At this time, there are no research studies testing the impact of urine drug testing, so parents must rely on common sense and carefully consider the pros and cons of such testing before they engage it.

The pros of these tests include:

• potentially discouraging and preventing substance use and all of its potential problems simply by doing the monitoring;
• clear communication of your views about substance use and your expectations of your child;
• having the opportunity to catch a problem early;
• giving your teenager a nice "out" during tricky social situations: "No, my parents drug test me."

The cons include:

• the awkwardness of drug testing, which can communicate a lack of trust;
• the possibility that a teen will switch to other substances that are harder to detect, such as acid, alcohol, or synthetic cannabinoids.

There is no easy answer, and parents need to decide what works best for their family. However, testing is often the wise, if difficult, path to pursue when there is a strong suspicion of substance use or a history of it. This is especially true during phases of active medical treatment, when privacy laws often prohibit doctors from sharing test results with parents. If your teen is in substance treatment, parents cannot rely on the therapist to notify them when their child uses drugs, because that would violate the legal mandates protecting a teen's confidentiality.

Whether your child is or isn't using, clean drug screens can be connected to rewards, such as a shopping date, and privileges, such as a one-hour extension of curfew.

If parents decide to conduct drug testing, here are some thoughts about how to do it:

Use only tests that have received approval from the U.S. Food and Drug Administration. This is indicated on the product packaging, and the precision of these tests is described on the FDA's website.[10]

Choose the type of specimen to be tested. Hair is less invasive than urine and provides information about drug use during the last one hundred or more days—but it is more expensive to test and not available in instant form. The specimen needs to be sent to a laboratory for analysis.

Saliva is also less invasive than urine, but it too is more expensive and provides information about substance use for no more than seven days.

Urine is the least expensive to test and also the most well studied. However, this testing is more invasive and easier to cheat. Parents who use urine testing should check the urine color, temperature, and specific gravity to make sure it is not diluted. They also should ask their teens to turn their pants pockets inside out and take off any heavy sweatshirts, jackets, or other clothing with pockets before providing the sample.

Pick the best place to test. If parents want to do drug testing but have difficulty conducting a test at home, or if they want a special kind of drug test, then commercial drug-testing companies may be helpful. Clients simply go to a testing facility and provide a sample under appropriate supervision. Results often can be accessed online.

If substance abuse has been confirmed, having a third-party test—whether conducted in a medical setting or at a testing facility—is smart, said Jo McGuire, who has served on the national board of directors of the Drug and Alcohol Testing Industry Association, or DATIA, which promotes professional standards for drug-testing professionals and facilities. DATIA's website includes a searchable database to help people find certified testing companies. Parents should take their children only to facilities that can guarantee a medical review officer or certified technician is on staff and available to explain a test's results.

"I can't tell you how many times the kids we would see would be caught trying to use urine they got from a sibling or friend," she said. "Their moms and dads thought their substance treatment was going so well, when it was really going nowhere.

"Parents should insist on drug testing by a third party because they need a baseline to know what, exactly, they're dealing with," she continued. "A home test typically just gives a yes-or-no result, while a reputable facility with certified testers can report drug levels, let you know if your child isn't taking a medicine as prescribed, and tell you exactly how much levels are going down to help ensure someone is getting off a specific drug or drugs."

Insight from the World of Recovery

"My parents are great people who told me that walking down the drug path was a bad idea, but they just never showed me there was another, better way to do *my* life," said Joe G., a nineteen-year-old in Saint Louis, Missouri, who tried marijuana for the first time at age fourteen. "They were always there. They were at every big event. They wanted to be part of my life. I knew logically that they loved me, and they told me so outright. But then we would sit down, and there were never these big, open-minded conversations. It was more like, 'No, this is the way it has to be, and stop arguing with me.' They always had my best interests in mind, but it was to a degree that it felt controlling and fear-based rather than rooted in nurturing someone into a better life.

"At home and school, I heard, 'Don't do this, and don't do that,' but I wanted to know why, and all I got was, 'Because I said so.' I wanted to know what the hell I was supposed to do instead to have the friends I wanted: they were the cool people who were older, had lots of friends themselves, and seemed to have everything they wanted and a lot of fun. All I knew was that my dad was from this really small community, and he'd never been exposed to all of the things I was, and, well, what could he possibly know? And my mom? She was just trying to keep me from doing whatever I wanted—or so I believed at the time.

"So kids need alternatives, and I'm talking about a lot more than finding things to do. I'm talking about something much deeper that helps them find who they really are and what that means. You can't just tell them, you have to show them. It takes more work, and it's not the path of least resistance, but it's what pays off the most—because when kids find that thing, that passion, that better way to live? They won't do drugs.

"All of the awful actions people make when they're doing drugs are motivated by something deeper within themselves. I wasn't making bad decisions just because I was smoking pot. Smoking pot was a bad decision—and it was just one of many bad decisions I was making. My big problem was really that I had no concept of internal worth. I didn't know there was even a force within me to tap into for good. Everything that led to my happiness came from outside of me—party invitations, clothes, cars, people, whatever was shallow. If someone had said, 'Instead of doing drugs at school, sit with people who really care about you,' or 'Stop trying to win the acceptance of people who are not going to accept you,' I think those things would have made a huge difference to me, because I was like a lot of people who lose themselves—and loathe themselves—in our world of constant comparisons and putdowns. We're the ones who think we've found self-worth in what turns out to be one of the deadliest forms of superficiality and artificiality out there.

"For people who step over that line, including me, it's because they've really stopped caring, and they've decided that nothing matters, even themselves.

"Society makes it so easy for us to fall for all of this. As generations have passed, we have integrated drug and alcohol use with just about everything. When there's a concert, the pot comes out. When the county fair or a ballgame happens, people get trashed. We have to think differently about fellowship and community and fun and enjoying ourselves—and respecting ourselves and others. We need more people who are willing to sacrifice lower forms of pleasure for the betterment of community. When I got sober, I had to learn that I could listen to music and not drink and that I could stay up really late and not smoke.

"Above all we have to teach people to genuinely love themselves. I wish I hadn't had to experience all that I have, but now I've found a better way of life—and I understand how to embrace it—I don't want to go back."

DISCUSSION QUESTIONS

- *How can you make any substances in your home less accessible to your children and their friends?*
- *How can you demonstrate the joy of "earned" or "natural" highs to your children—and encourage them to pursue their own?*
- *Can you list three ways your child would like to spend time with you this month?*
- *Following the general, age-appropriate guidelines provided, how will you explain the harms of drug use to your child?*
- *If you and your child were to build your team together, who would be on it and why?*
- *How have you and your child planned to make you the "bad guy" when tricky social situations come up?*

3

WHAT TO DO WHEN YOU LEARN YOUR CHILD IS USING DRUGS

Learning your son or daughter has tried, or is actively using, substances typically prompts a rush of difficult emotions. This chapter provides practical tips on how to approach everything from first-time use to full-fledged addiction.

Regardless of whether the drug use is new or has evolved into substance dependence, parents often feel guilty, thinking they did something—or didn't do something—to cause the behavior. They typically react in a couple of ways. The first is to pretend nothing has happened, because saying something also would force the parent to face his or her feelings of inadequacy, guilt, and/or failure. The second common reaction is profound betrayal that erupts as sadness and anger. Both camps of parents often become anxious and sicken themselves with worry.

These are all normal reactions—but they can quickly become a part of the problem, which is substance use, period. A parent's feelings of anger, embarrassment, fear, guilt, inadequacy, powerlessness, or shame are not going to convince adolescents to stop using substances. They even can drive youth further into the world of substance abuse and alienation from family and true friends.

Remember: the most important tool you have to influence your adolescent is your positive relationship with him or her. When a child has used a drug or has a substance problem, those positive feelings are going to suffer a blow—and their restoration might take a while. Parents who move most quickly to a healthy and effective place from which they can deal with their child's substance use are those parents who have addressed their own mindset first.

That mindset is firmly rooted in what is known as the three Cs of Al-Anon, an organization focused on helping family and friends of problem drinkers. They are, "You did not Cause the addiction. You cannot Control it. You cannot Cure it." While these principles were originally developed for family members of people with full-fledged addiction, they also apply to parents whose children are experimenting for the first time and to parents who know their kids use alcohol and drugs occasionally without exhibiting signs of addiction. Parents who embrace the three Cs quickly ("You did not Cause the drug use. You cannot Control the drug use. You cannot Cure the drug use.") become a part of the solutions that encourage their children to stop using drugs and alcohol. These parents relinquish:

- **anger**. Whether it's a quiet simmer or a good, old-fashioned stack-blowing aimed at specific family members or at the larger world that seems to encourage drug abuse at every turn, anger isn't helping. It might be justified, but it isn't helping. It does, however, give parents plenty of excuses to do nothing about their own responsibilities—and that's not helping, either.
- **guilt**. Parents often get stuck in the notion that their child's bad behavior is solely a reflection of their effectiveness as parents. It isn't. Parents who let go of guilt recognize that they shouldn't blame themselves for, or otherwise own, every choice their children make, or when their children fail to meet their expectations, or for how their children "turned out" compared to everyone else's kids.
- **fear**. Being fearful about what could happen to a drug-using child is reasonable—but acting out of fear often is not. Parents who relinquish fear no longer care what others may be thinking about them or their child. They understand how to hold their ground against substance use because they're confident parents who know the latest brain development science, believe in what they're doing, and know they're not failures at life because their child has made poor choices. These parents also have learned that it's important to deal in reality rather than in the false assumptions of a runaway mind, which can cause paralyzing fear. In this case,

reality is that a teen is using substances and may be disrupting a home or posing harm to others. Imagining and ruminating on what anyone else might think or do about that isn't helpful.

- **shame and embarrassment.** When parents truly understand that they didn't cause their child's drug use or problem, they often let go of the shame and embarrassment that have driven them to hide from the issue and/or hide the issue from others. Substance use and substance use disorder are what they are—and they develop over time as outlined in the first chapter of this book. The sooner parents acknowledge and address issues directly, the sooner they can foster the positive relationship that encourages their teen to live a healthy life.

- **control of things they never really controlled anyway.** Parents understandably want to protect their children from harm, but that doesn't mean they can control their teens or entire environments in which their teens interact daily. What parents can control is themselves, what happens in their homes, and what happens on their dime.

So now let's explore what it's going to take to have productive discussions that help everyone achieve their desired outcomes.

While it's much easier said than done, remaining calm really does work wonders for everyone. Research shows yelling, screaming, crying, laying down guilt trips, and having emotional breakdowns are not only unhelpful but also probably harmful.[1] After all, adolescents frequently gravitate wherever they can get attention, whether it's positive or negative. Conflict can actually reinforce behavior you're trying to discourage.

Strive to strengthen your relationship, or "attachment," with your child by loving, listening—and also by making yourself heard. One model to consider is Attachment Communication Training, or ACT, developed by Terry M. Levy, Ph.D., and Michael Orlans, M.A., of the Evergreen Psychotherapy Center and Attachment Treatment and Training Institute in Evergreen, Colorado.

First, ACT establishes these ground rules for communication:

- No blaming or criticism.

- If it is impossible to talk without destructive emotion, the conversation stops.
- There is no contempt, defensiveness, or stonewalling.
- There is no interrupting.
- Everyone must recognize that there will be times to agree to disagree. Everyone should be allowed to have his or her own feelings and viewpoints.
- Discussions must happen once a week for consistency and practice.
- When there is no resolution to a serious problem, everyone agrees to see a therapist about it.

Next, ACT identifies the elements of effective communication and destructive communication:

Effective communicators:

- are empathetic and validate others' thoughts and feelings (they communicate understanding even if they do not agree).
- listen and paraphrase others' thoughts and feelings.
- give clear, honest, and immediate feedback without being judgmental or blaming.
- ask for feedback.
- maintain a style of speaking that matches the content of what's being said (for example, sarcasm is strongly discouraged).
- share thoughts and feelings.
- remain focused on a single issue or theme.
- ask clarifying questions.
- are open-minded and reserve judgment.
- are assertive, not aggressive.
- seek to keep the intent of their remarks in line with the impact they could have on others.
- are aware of nonverbal messages, such as eye contact, body language, and tone of voice (in other words, they are willing to stop talking and start listening when their child's body language indicates frustration).
- quickly edit imprecise comments to avoid conflict and provocation.

- halt conversation when helpful (for example, when people need to cool down).
- are committed to positive, constructive communication even when upset, angry, or frustrated.
- give whole messages that express observations, thoughts, feelings, and needs.

Destructive communicators:

- use the following techniques: labeling ("You liar!"); predicting ("You won't really follow through on this."); personalization (being offended by things that are not personal); generalizing (taking one small concept and assuming it applies to everything); distracting (shifting the focus of the conversation unnecessarily); kitchen-sinking (bringing up minor issues); cross-complaining ("Oh, well, what about the time you . . . ?"); yes-butting ("Yeah, but . . . "); placating (telling people what they want to hear without planning to actually do anything); mind reading ("You don't really care what I'm saying."); and comparing people's hardships ("You think you have it hard. What about me?").
- are judgmental.
- focus on the negative instead of the positive.
- use polarizing language or knowingly "push others' buttons."
- don't listen or validate. They focus only on themselves.
- complain, nag, criticize, insult, attack, blame, and threaten.
- pseudo listen. They placate, rehearse their comebacks, and actively avoid conflicts to seek approval.
- interrupt.
- dig in their heels to their position and create "win-lose" standoffs.
- are vague and general.
- are rude and impolite.
- air old resentments.
- do not halt heated conversations.

Having clear ground rules and a good mindset will also help you find the right words at the right time. ACT also provides guidance for sharing and listening. Here's how Levy and Orlans break down the give-and-take:

Sharing Skills

- Make statements rather than ask questions. (For example, "I would like to talk about this" instead of "Why don't we talk about this?")
- Take responsibility for your own perceptions by making "I" statements rather than by saying "you." ("I'm frustrated" instead of "You are rude.")
- Be specific, concise, and honest. Do not hint, expect others to read your mind, or say what you "don't want."
- Share your thoughts and feelings: they are separate.
- Be aware of your verbal and nonverbal messaging.
- Be assertive and positive. Do not criticize, blame, attack, or complain.

Listening Skills

- Relax and absorb. Do not censor or rehearse your rebuttal.
- Have a nonjudgmental attitude. Listen for what's right, not just what's wrong.
- Be empathetic. Try to place yourself in your discussion partner's position.
- Send accepting, understanding, supportive messages—and validate that you've heard what has been said. ("I can understand why you feel that way.")
- Be aware of self: nonverbal behavior, such as eye contact, tone of voice, body positioning, thoughts, and feelings.
- Listen on two different levels. Listening for content will help you understand thoughts and feelings, while listening for the style of delivery will help you understand the context and emotion behind what is said.
- Give feedback indicating messages are received—even if your confirmation is nonverbal. ("I hear that you want to have a later curfew.")

ACT also describes common "blocks to listening" that lead to breakdowns in communication:

- Comparing: self to other, who is better, who is experiencing more pain, who is right.

- Mind reading: trying to figure out what another person is "really" thinking and feeling without ever taking at face value what the person has said he or she is thinking and feeling. Mind readers also make assumptions about how people are reacting to them.
- Rehearsing: focusing on preparing your next comment instead of listening. People who are rehearsing often appear to be interested, but their minds are elsewhere.
- Filtering: selective listeners absorb only those things they want to hear and reject the things they don't.
- Judging: creating labels and prejudging others promotes knee-jerk reactions.
- Dreaming: triggering chains of private associations in your own thoughts—and not paying attention.
- Identifying: linking—and referencing—everything to your own experience. (No, it's not all about you.)
- Advising: trying to problem-solve and offer suggestions.
- Sparring: arguing and debating—and generally working to find things with which to disagree. This may involve criticism, battles for control, and the discounting of one's self (inability to receive a compliment).
- Being right: going to any length to avoid being wrong; unable to handle criticism or suggestions or to acknowledge mistakes. (Admit your mistakes, move on, and pick and choose your battles.)
- Derailing: changing the subject and/or using humor to avoid serious discussion.
- Placating: acting pleasant, supportive, and agreeable—when you aren't.

Try also to root your discussion in the basic principles of nonviolent communication.[2] We'll unpack some of these approaches in more detail in chapter 5, where we cover specific family objectives during therapy sessions. However, these are the steps recommended for initial conversations after you've confirmed your teen is using drugs and alcohol.

Step 1: Make observations, not evaluations. Examples of observations are "My son's room smelled like marijuana yesterday and today"; "I found four beer cans in my daughter's backpack, and the day before $20 went missing from my wallet"; and "My son's grades are down, he's not playing basketball as often as he used to, and he's more irritable this week than usual." Examples of evaluations are "My son is a drug addict"; "My daughter is always irritable"; and "My son is lazy."

Step 2: Recognize the difference between your feelings and your thoughts. Expressing your feelings is a powerful tool for resolving conflict. It shows your humanity, humility, and vulnerability—all of which can break down relationship barriers. Examples of feelings are "I feel disappointed"; "I feel hurt"; and "I feel angry and scared." Those are clearly defined emotions. Examples of thoughts are "I feel betrayed by my son"; "I feel like a failure"; "I feel like my daughter doesn't appreciate everything we've done for her"; and "I feel like grounding you forever." See how these thoughts are a mixture of emotion, evaluation, and judgment that assign beliefs, blame, and action?

Step 3: Express your needs or requests. This step is especially important because you're more likely to have your needs met when you clearly say what they are. You must not assume people can read your mind, "automatically know," or even guess what you need. Common needs parents have in relationship to their children are appreciation, closeness, honesty, respect, safety, support, trust, and understanding. If you are feeling angry, hurt, sad, or upset with your teenager, there is a good chance one of these relational needs is not being met. As you speak, try to start with an "I" statement, which is tough to argue with because it focuses on you.

Now let's focus on how to put these approaches into action. The ACT communication method involves the six following steps:

- **Use your sharing skills.**
- **Use your listening skills.**
- **Restate.** After the sharer is finished speaking, the listener should restate what was heard. You might begin by saying, "I heard you say . . ."
- **Give feedback.** After restating, the sharer should give the listener feedback on the accuracy of his or her listening. If the listener restated accurately, the sharer can reward with verbal or nonverbal appreciation. If the restating is inaccurate or partially accurate, the sharer must clarify. For example, "No, I didn't say what you heard, so I would like to try again."
- **Process.** Take time to talk about the give-and-take of your discussion. Use the same method to consider the following questions:

1. What was it like for you both to communicate with each other in this manner?
2. How did you feel with you discussion partner as "sharer" and as "listener"?
3. In what ways will your relationship be enhanced by communicating in this way?
4. What are some of the issues you would like to discuss using this way of communicating?

- **Reverse roles.** Make time for the sharer to become the listener and vice versa so both parties have a chance to practice sharing and listening. As the adult, you will have to model both behaviors for a while before you can expect your teen to be able to do this.

At first, using a method or formula to converse may feel unnatural, inauthentic, stilted, and even stifling, but with practice, discussion really does become easier, more rewarding, and more effective.

Here are some simple examples of ways to frame conversations:

Recommended: "I am sad about your drug use because I want you to grow up healthy and to reach your maximum potential."

Trap: "I feel like a failure because I didn't teach you right from wrong." Or, worse, "You use drugs and don't appreciate anything we've done for you." In the first trap, the parent is not expressing a true feeling and is making a judgment about right and wrong. In the second trap, the parent makes several, sweeping assumptions and judgments.

Recommended: "It must be hard not to use marijuana if it feels like everyone else is using. However, I'm sad you're using because I want you to grow strong. Tell me what marijuana does for you and how I could help you accomplish the same things in ways that don't jeopardize your health and safety." This statement begins with empathetic validation and expresses a feeling and a need.

Trap: "I want you to stop using drugs." While this is tempting to say, it is frequently very unhelpful and makes teens defensive and more determined to engage the behavior you want to extinguish.

When talking with adolescents about issues related to substance use—a common one is curfew—consider these recommendations and traps:

Recommended: "I'm disappointed that you've come home late because I wanted to get a good night's sleep," or "I am upset that you didn't take out the garbage because I need help getting everything done around the house."

Traps: "You let me down because you said you would do something and didn't," or "I get upset when you're so lazy," or "I'm disappointed that you're home late because I want you to respect me." Note that the first trap uses a judgment and does not express a clear feeling or need. The second trap makes a judgment instead of an observation and also does not express a need. The third trap starts out strong with a feeling—but it ends with an unclear request. It is very important for requests to be precise: "Please be home by 10 p.m."

Expressing a precise emotion followed by a precise need is much more likely to lead to an honest and productive exchange. While this is the ideal approach to communication in this situation, there is no guarantee that it produces immediate, positive results. Keep trying and don't give up. You'll get better each time you work at it—and your child will slowly realize you're trying a different approach. Persistence is the key. Too often, parents say, "But I tried this, and it didn't work." Unfortunately, change takes time and persistent effort.

THE TREATMENT PROVIDER'S PERSPECTIVE

"Parental guilt and ego are very big problems that get in the way of a kid's substance recovery," said Terry Levy from his offices in Evergreen, Colorado. "Parents often say, 'The divorce did it,' 'My husband doesn't pay attention,' or 'My wife is a control freak,' or 'It was those people down the street. We should have known their son was bad for ours.' They focus on external factors and tie everything to their own ego.

"Then, on the flip side, there are parents who blame their substance-using kid for causing all of their personal, marital, or family problems. 'You're the reason we're divorcing,' or 'Dad doesn't know what to do with you, and you've driven Mom to worry herself to death,' or 'You're the reason I can't focus at work and am getting into trouble with my boss.'

"We spend a lot of time trying to help people own only what they need to own and fix what they need to fix. When roles and responsibilities are confused, and everyone blames someone else for their problems, it's hard to get to the root of a problem. Frankly, I often see that parents are having problems that have nothing to do with their kid's addiction. It's unfair of them to blame their kids for those problems, but the kid's addiction has become a great scapegoat that helps them avoid addressing their own issues.

"That's why parents often need to be in therapy while their kids are struggling with substance use disorder. Once their kid is in recovery, these parents are still going to have problems—and they won't be able to blame their kid's drug use for them anymore."

The adolescent brain thinks differently than the adult brain. As we covered in chapter 1, parents should keep in mind that the adolescent brain has not fully developed its skills for reading other people's emotions, reasoning, self-control, and thinking ahead.[3] For parents of teens who are using substances weekly or more often, the adolescent, addicted brain is especially challenging to handle.

Engaging in thoughtful and truthful discussion with a drug-using teen can be incredibly difficult. Depending on his or her drug of choice and frequency of use, you might be trying to engage someone who is perpetually under the influence—or, as Mike Weiland, the treatment provider in Missouri, likes to say, "operating under foreign management."

After all, drugs allow users to create for themselves new realities that are so enticing they don't care about the various problems disrupting their lives and those of everyone around them. Parents fighting, bad grades, relationship troubles, nagging bosses—poof! Those problems and many more disappear with another drink, another smoke, another pill, another hit, another chemical—or so it would appear.

In reality, the problems loom larger than ever because when drugs begin to control a developing mind, they also stunt an adolescent's emotional development. Drug-abusing teens rely on chemicals to help them deal with, and often avoid, life's difficulties and challenges—while their sober peers continue developing the maturity they'll eventually need to handle adult problems and stressors as adults should.

"I tell parents all the time that they have this experientially advanced, intellectually twisted, and emotionally immature person on their hands," Weiland said. "If they want to know how to deal with a particular problem, I always ask how old their kid was when he started using, because that's basically where he's going to be emotionally, and they'll need to adjust their approach accordingly."

As if that's not enough of a challenge for parents, Weiland underscores the rapidly growing disconnection often observed between a drug-abusing adolescent's emotional and intellectual development. While drugs may hinder emotional maturity, they don't necessarily cripple intellect—so the gap between what substance-abusing teens know they should do and feel they should do runs wide and deep.

"That gap is exacerbated by exposure to nonstop media that feed teenagers a lot of ridiculous information about what is essentially a brain-destroying epidemic they think is good for them," he added.

It's appropriate to challenge a young drug user's bogus beliefs about how fantastic and/or harmless his drug use is—but it's also very important to recognize that these conversations often turn into unproductive arguments.

Insight from the World of Recovery

"Y'know those movies where you see the little angel and the little demon sitting on someone's shoulder, whispering in their ear?" asked Nell C., a twenty-year-old in substance recovery in Columbia, Missouri. "I knew what the little angel wanted me to do, but I was powerless because I needed drugs. I needed them because I couldn't deal with how I felt. There were a lot of girls around me at school who could deal with not doing well in a game or some other problem, but that wasn't me. It was like nothing was ever good enough, and I was very hard on myself. I still remember how upset I would get and how I just wanted to be numb because I couldn't let myself feel sad. I knew all along that there was some underlying thing I needed to deal with, but there was no way I would have stopped getting high unless by a power greater than me. I didn't want to get out of that world of getting high—but there was definitely something that wanted me out. It was my mom's tireless efforts to reach me and all of the patience she showed me that got me to that first intervention."

PARENTS WHO HAVE BEEN THERE

"When all of this started with my son, can you believe I worked in school safety?" asked Jo McGuire, a Colorado Springs drug-testing expert whose son still struggles with addiction. "I was the prevention queen—but at that time, I was focused primarily on other teen problems. I was big on talking about everything with my children, but drugs and alcohol were such big no-nos and so taboo that I just knew my kids would never touch them. When I look back now, I realize that what I didn't do in my communication was to explain why drugs were not healthy choices.

"So by the time I realized my son had a problem and that I needed to have more conversations with him, I could see immediately how wrapped up he was in drug messaging. 'It's good for me,' he'd say. 'It's healthy, and it's an herb that is one of the best medicines in the world.' He told me I was the one speaking out of paranoia and merely parroting what the government says.

"At first, I would engage in arguments, and I would always kick myself for doing that because it's just dumb to argue with drug logic. In those moments, I also realized I wasn't loving or teaching him."

"We're still trying to figure out how to make observations," said Lisa Taylor, a Colorado Springs mother who continues to grapple with her son's addiction. "Once you have determined what's going on, you also have to understand that you're not going to be able to speak rationally with someone who is irrational. Always tell yourself this, and never let up. At first I would say, 'Look at your grades. You are no longer in control. Marijuana is controlling you.' But then I also had to come to a place where I could just understand that he's not going to get it, at least not right now. When a parent can finally reach that state of awareness, it's like having a huge weight lifted from your shoulders."

DISCUSSION QUESTIONS

- *What triggers your anger?*
- *How does your child's drug use make you feel, and what needs will you communicate to him or her?*

- *How should you adjust your language to avoid the discussion "traps" listed in this chapter?*
- *When and how can you relinquish your anger, guilt, fear, shame, and embarrassment?*

4

WHEN TO SEEK TREATMENT AND WHAT TO LOOK FOR IN IT

When parents discover a teen has used drugs or alcohol, they have a lot to think about, and this chapter aims to help them navigate the decision-making process.

We've already established that it's important to stay calm and positive—which not only helps to keep your family relationships intact, but also to assess the situation accurately. There are some important first questions to get answered so you can determine next steps:

- Was this substance use one-time experimentation or a habit?
- Is there dangerous behavior in any way connected to the substance use, such as driving while under the influence, having unprotected sex under the influence, or distribution of substances?
- How is your adolescent doing academically, athletically, socially, and at home? Are you noticing any negative change in behavior?
- Are there mental health issues in play? Do you think you're observing low self-esteem, anxiety, or depression?
- Do you suspect your adolescent is lying or stretching truth? Listen for the improbable and unlikely: "I was holding the pipe in my backpack for a friend." Now is a good time to be highly skeptical—and to know that early substance users are typically very cautious about hiding their substance use. It's usually only when a problem has progressed that they carry substances and parapher-

nalia recklessly. When in doubt, err on the side of getting an evaluation with a specialist.

Let's start at the mild end of the spectrum. If you suspect one-time experimentation and are fairly certain there are no co-occurring problems, you and your adolescent probably do not need outside help. Instead you could increase your monitoring and make your child earn back his or her privileges. If, however, this appears to be a one-time event in an adolescent who does have co-occurring problems, such as a decline in functioning, depression, and irritability, you should seek professional help.

If you learn your adolescent has tried substances a couple of times but has no obvious, co-occurring problems, you have a difficult decision to make. You could increase monitoring and require privileges be earned back, or you could seek an initial consult with a licensed professional to help you assess the situation further, because there is a risk the substance use is more of a problem than you know. Delaying treatment could worsen the substance problem. Parents really must trust their instincts and make the best decision they can with the information they have.

If you believe your adolescent has tried substances more than a couple of times, seek professional help regardless of whether there are co-occurring problems. Too often, adolescents convince their parents and themselves that they should be allowed to use marijuana, alcohol, tobacco, and other substances as long as they get good grades and stay out of trouble. Aside from the potential harm to brain development outlined in chapter 1, this is dangerous. For example, one in six adolescents who try marijuana before the age of eighteen develops a marijuana use disorder—and this risk rises with each use.[1] Err on the side of getting an evaluation with a specialist.

INSIGHT FROM THE WORLD OF RECOVERY

"I have never met anyone addicted to alcohol or drugs who didn't have another problem first," said Joe G., a nineteen-year-old in recovery in Saint Louis. "I'm not saying the substances aren't a big deal, because they are. It's just that I haven't met anyone who has been able to abstain from use without dealing with all of those underlying issues. What I had to realize for my own good is that chronic, habitual users of any mind-altering chemical are usually trying to escape something—and they have to dig that out and face it.

"But getting to that point takes time, and when parents are over-reacting to everything instead of responding reasonably, it is very easy to shut them out. Parents shouldn't instantly assume everything is just falling apart when it's not, and they shouldn't make everything so cataclysmic. They need to be concerned enough to do something but not so angry enough that they always appear one step away from sending their kid to live on the streets.

"Everyone figuring into this equation needs to be open to honest appraisal, and you want only someone who is well informed and experienced in dealing with substance abuse and addiction and in helping young people."

All of this begs the question of what kind of treatment to seek—and from whom to seek it. It is mission-critical to find treatment that meets a young person's unique needs, because a good-to-great fit is what encourages someone to stick with treatment. When people don't engage in treatment long enough or in honest and meaningful ways, they're not likely to reach the overarching goals of stopping drug use and living successfully within family, community, and the workplace.

THE TREATMENT PROVIDER'S PERSPECTIVE

"This is definitely one of those times when parents need to understand that this decision really isn't all about them," said certified addictions counselor Josh Azevedo, director of The Pathway Program in Phoenix, Arizona, where he has worked with hundreds of youth who feel they can relate to him especially well because of his own teen battles with addiction and decades of sobriety. "So look for a fit for your child. You might be happy with people wearing ties and white coats, but what is your kid going to respond to?"

"Around here, we look like the Allman Brothers and not a counseling staff for a reason," said ponytailed Crossroads Program director Mike Weiland as he stroked the long, brown beard that has become his trademark. "I don't chase symptoms; I'm after root causes. I meet with parents first to understand what's happening from their perspective. Then I meet with their child to understand things as they see it. When I see a clear problem, I want to attract young people to recovery—a new reality. I want them to see the exciting and loving reality that is better than getting high. I want them to see other young people, and some of the fun we can have together sober on Friday nights. Cool people who can communicate with kids? They're key."

The National Institute on Drug Abuse (NIDA) recommends parents evaluate treatment options based on the answers to four key questions:[2]

Does the program use treatments supported by scientific evidence? Examples include

- cognitive behavioral therapy, which seeks to help people "recognize, avoid and cope with the situations in which they are most likely to abuse drugs";
- motivational incentives, or the use of positive reinforcements, such as privileges and rewards, for remaining drug-free or participating in counseling sessions;
- motivational interviewing, which employs strategies to encourage "self-driven behavior" to stop drug use and perhaps enter treatment;
- integrated mental health–substance treatment, which concurrently addresses both the substance use disorder and mental health issues, such as depression and anxiety; and
- family treatment, which helps parents know how they can help their teen in the recovery process.

Does the program customize treatment to meet the needs of each patient? "No single treatment is right for everyone," NIDA says. "The best treatment addresses a person's various needs, not just his or her drug abuse."

Does the program adapt treatment as the patient's needs change? Treatment programs should be flexible enough to provide the varying combinations of services a patient needs. For example, built-in drug monitoring might need to be adjusted if relapse happens—or doesn't happen.

Is the duration of treatment sufficient? NIDA explains it well: "Research tells us that most addicted people need at least three months in treatment to really reduce or stop their drug use and that longer treatment times result in better outcomes. The best programs will measure progress and suggest plans for maintaining recovery. Recovery from drug addiction is a long-term process that often requires several episodes of treatment and ongoing support from family or community."

How do twelve-step or similar recovery programs fit into addiction treatment? Many clinicians encourage patients to participate in social-support groups focused on helping people with abstinence. For youth in substance recovery, these programs can be especially helpful to rebuild social connections and identify prosocial activities that encourage healthy living and foster the emotional development that was delayed by substance dependence.

With these overarching observations made, there are finer details to observe about treatment programs and treatment providers. Here are some general principles from the American Academy of Child and Adolescent Psychiatry's practice parameters for the "Assessment and Treatment of Children and Adolescents with Substance Use Disorders" and from NIDA's *Principles of Drug Addiction Treatment.*

Treatment should begin with a comprehensive, initial assessment conducted by a qualified clinician. This clinician should spend one to two hours alone with your adolescent, obtaining information about the following:

- substance use (which substances, frequency of use, quantity of use, display of any symptoms of substance use disorder);
- psychiatric symptoms (anger, anxiety, attention deficit hyperactivity disorder, depression, psychosis);
- medical history; and
- psychosocial history (family relationships, peers, hobbies, strengths).

But wait. Who is a "qualified" clinician, and how can parents find these professionals?

Qualified clinicians will have professional experience and formal training in the treatment of adolescent addictions. Frankly, when it comes to addiction treatment, you need a specialist.

Primary care physicians and general mental health practitioners may be helpful to parents when they're trying to determine whether suspicions should be followed up by a specialist—but they are often quickly overwhelmed by the evaluation and treatment of adolescent substance use disorders. It is not unusual for them to be fooled by the disorder and unaware of important aspects of addiction treatment, to be too confrontational with the adolescent, or to have trouble managing the confidentiality necessary to perform the evaluation and deliver treatment.

All of this is understandable given that so few physicians in the United States know how to identify and treat patients with substance abuse problems. The vast majority of the nation's medical schools do not require a single course on addiction. Fewer than ten do, according to the Philadelphia-based Treatment Research Institute.

Also concerning are programs claiming that computerized or pen-and-paper questionnaires diagnose, and even treat, patients with substance use disorders. While such tools can be helpful adjuncts, they should never take the place of meeting face-to-face with a skillful and qualified clinician. There are simply too many complexities, nuances, and judgment calls in the assessment and treatment of adolescents with substance use disorders for a computer to understand.

So look for truly qualified clinicians. Some programs team master's-level therapists and child psychiatrists to conduct evaluations. Some physicians work in tandem with treatment providers offering substance abuse counseling, twelve-step programming, and an array of social activities.

These varying tag teams allow for counselors and therapists to develop and maintain rapport from the start and for a physician to obtain a thorough assessment of possible co-occurring physical and psychiatric disorders. This level of attention is important because about 80 percent of adolescents presenting for substance treatment have a co-occurring psychiatric disorder.[3]

PARENTS WHO HAVE BEEN THERE

"Losing my beautiful son, Shane, to suicide in January 2012, when he was twenty-five, has devastated my family," said Lori Robinson, who lives in Southern California. "Looking back now, we were all so naive.

"My husband and I have never used drugs, and we raised our sons in a drug-free home. Except for one time we knew Shane had tried alcohol, it never occurred to us that our smart, loving, and hardworking son would ever touch other drugs. Later we learned he started using cannabis when he was nineteen. He eventually told his father and me a high school girlfriend introduced him to it and that all of his friends assured him it was harmless. He naively believed them when they all told him there was nothing to worry about, that it was just a plant, an ancient and precious herb, and not even a drug. He really managed to hide his use from us—and even when we found out about it, he insisted we had nothing to worry about. We believed him.

"But then came Shane's first psychotic break just after he'd turned twenty-three. He spent ten days in the hospital—and during that time, the admitting, general psychiatrist and other staff diagnosed Shane with bipolar disorder, but they *minimized the effects of the marijuana use.* When Shane was released, we had trouble finding a knowledgeable, outpatient psychiatrist for him. We stopped seeing one who actually told us 'a little marijuana won't hurt.' We found another who focused intently on the medications used to control his bipolar disorder—but who failed to treat what we began to recognize as marijuana addiction.

"It is still hard for me to believe that none of these medical professionals had a clue about what I have devoted my life to learning in the months since my beautiful boy's death: marijuana is strongly associated with psychosis, which can happen to young people with a family like ours, a family with no medical history of this condition. I confess that it is hard for me not to be angry when I think about all of the doctors, nurses, and health-care professionals who were just so ignorant about this drug and who arrogantly dismissed even the possibility that marijuana was a contributing factor to our son's deteriorating mental health.

"I am convinced that if Shane had seen a doctor who truly specialized in adolescent addiction—and specifically marijuana addiction—he would be alive today."

Treatment providers are usually in the best position to judge the care of other treatment providers. Ask your family practitioner for local referrals or contact the state chapter of the American Academy of Child and Adolescent Psychiatry (www.aacap.org) or the American Academy of Pediatrics (www.aap.org).

If these routes don't result in a good fit, here are other possible resources:

- School psychologists, nurses, social workers, and guidance counselors
- Clergy and pastoral counselors working in faith-based organizations
- Your state's office of behavioral health, which may offer a guide to qualified clinicians
- The Substance Abuse and Mental Health Services National Registry of Evidence-Based Practices and Programs (NREPP) website: wwww.nrepp.samhsa.gov. Please note that this website is a good place to start your search, but the information on the website may be dated.
- Paid consultants. Some families benefit from seeking services from consultants who specialize in helping parents identify and place their adolescents in treatment programs. Some of these consultants may receive benefits or bonuses for making certain referrals. Always be aware of their potential conflicts of interest.

As you evaluate treatment possibilities, ask providers if they could put you in touch with other parents whose children have been in their program. Also make sure you understand how group meetings are structured—and avoid any program that combines adolescents and adults or that is open to such a wide array of needs that it would be difficult for your child's addiction to be addressed.

Parents should look for a provider who understands and respects the adolescent's confidentiality. Your adolescent's treatment must be confidential. Unless there is serious suicidal ideation, homicidal ideation, or child/elder abuse, the information an adolescent shares with the clinician must be kept private unless the adolescent agrees for the clinician to share the information. The adolescent gets to choose what information to share, with whom it may be shared, how it may be shared, and when it may be shared—and he or she also may revoke this consent to share information at any time.

All of this means parents should not rely on the clinician to tell them about their child's substance use or whether there has been a relapse. *Parents need to continue their own monitoring at home even if their adolescent is in treatment.* Privacy laws do not prevent parents from telling clinicians about worrisome events, but they do prohibit clinicians from sharing information about an adolescent without appropriate permission. So if you have information that you want your adolescent's clinician to know, pick up the phone and leave a voicemail or send an e-mail. Then tell your teen you made that contact, because it is better for them to know directly from you than to learn about your outreach from their counselor or therapist. Privacy laws do not prohibit clinicians from sharing with your teen what you communicated.

There are many reasons treatment needs to be confidential. Research shows that when assured of confidentiality, adolescents are honest about their substance use.[4] Honesty, in turn, is necessary for a successful treatment. There are also ethical and legal reasons for confidentiality, which were established to protect basic human rights.

However, it's true that confidentiality poses challenges. How are parents to know if a child is getting better? How are they to know how to help? How can they know if treatment providers are trustworthy and competent? Isn't it unfair that parents typically pay for treatment and yet do not know the details of what happened in session?

These are valid concerns. Parents should raise them during the initial session, giving clinicians a chance to explain how they'll be addressed. For example, parents may get to participate in some sessions to understand what has transpired in treatment and how they could be helpful to continued progress. Parents may also receive information when a treatment doesn't appear to be working and other, more intensive treatments are needed. It's important for parents to be able to make inquiries early and often—and for these discussions to be in the open.

Parents also should work diligently to protect their child's privacy. They often debate about whom they should and shouldn't tell about the substance problem. There are two rules of thumb:

The first is to share only with people who genuinely can be helpful to the situation. Perhaps these people could help identify a qualified clinician. Maybe they could provide transportation or resources to cover the costs of treatment. If you're unsure about whether someone could be helpful to you, or how to ask for help, consult your child's treatment provider for advice.

The second rule is to tell as few people as possible—and to say something only after consulting with your child. Adolescents highly prize their privacy and are often embarrassed or ashamed easily.

GETTING YOUR ADOLESCENT TO THAT FIRST MEETING

It is highly common for young people to resist treatment. Very few adolescents want to get help for their emotional or behavioral problems. This is normal. The good news is that with motivational interviewing, which is explained in more detail later in this chapter, this resistance usually dissipates quickly.

The other good news is that baseline motivation for change does not predict adolescent substance treatment outcomes.[5] This is because good treatment does things to enhance an adolescent's motivation for positive change. So it bears repeating: *adolescents still benefit from, and should receive, treatment even if they do not initially want it.*

Parents often ask, "How do I get my child to treatment?" Young people almost always need some kind of encouragement from the adults around them. Sometimes it's enough for a parent simply to say, "You're going to treatment." Other times they must engage in a negotiation, such as, "If you want this privilege (think use of a car, cell phone, computer, curfew, privacy), you will go to treatment."

Remember that honesty really is the best policy. Be forthright about the nature of the first appointment. Don't lead your child to think you're going to a pediatrician for a general checkup when you're actually visiting a child psychiatrist who will ask specifically about the teen's substance use.

And frame the nature of your visit thoughtfully. "This is a doctor who will try to understand and help with anger, anxiety, depression, substance use, and whatever else might be troubling you." A motivational therapist will align his or her approach with those stated goals and desires.

Insight from the World of Recovery

"My parents gave me lots of chances," said Raymond N., a man in his early twenties who started smoking tobacco at age fourteen and moved on to marijuana only a few months later. "They caught me with various amounts of marijuana or paraphernalia and they would wig out, ground me, and take away the car—but they didn't make a call to the doctor for a while. I agree that seeking medical help is not the first thing parents should do, but I don't think it's a good idea to wait as long as my parents did, either. The sad thing here is that honestly, I am not sure when the right time to find help is.

"What I am sure of is that I spent five years getting loaded and being sneaky and manipulative. It became obvious that something was wrong with me mentally. I was acting out, getting into big fights over the littlest things, and my parents started asking why I was nineteen and acting like I was twelve. I got into this huge argument with my mom over the stupidest thing, and it escalated so much that she took my phone and car keys. She also looked and found texts that confirmed I had been doing drugs for years. That's when my parents really knew I needed help—and they'd been in denial.

"I fought them tooth and nail about going to that first meeting, but then the counselor talked with me for a while, and I had never, ever related with anyone like I did him. I had never heard anyone talk about drugs and addiction the way he did. I was fascinated—and I realized I hated my life and had nowhere to go but up. I was at the end of my rope."

"It was my senior year in high school. I had been getting high every day for about one and a half years at that point. I was smoking weed daily because I couldn't even feel normal anymore unless I was high," said twenty-year-old Nell C., who is now in substance recovery and working toward a college degree. "But that day, I started out with a friend who was a really bad influence. I took ecstasy and, when he offered, I snorted a little bit of heroin. It was my first time with that, and I didn't even know what was too much.

"I had already gotten permission from my mom to have dinner with friends that night, so I didn't go home at all. When I met everyone, we smoked marijuana—and I passed out. My friends had no idea what was going on, and they didn't know I was on ecstasy and heroin also.

"For two hours, I threw up and nodded out—and they were afraid to take me to the hospital because they were high. Even though I was unconscious, I can still remember thinking, 'I would rather die than have my mom find out I was doing drugs.'

"I actually made it home somehow and went back to school. Rumors about what happened started circulating, and it was a counselor with my Young Life group who confronted me. I lied to him about the nature of the drugs I used, but that didn't stop him from talking with my mom.

"The next day, it was my mom and my Young Life counselor who pulled me out of school early and announced the three of us were going to meet with this really nice woman I liked a lot. She is a family counselor I had seen, and when we were in her office, she explained that we were going to figure out what was true and not about where I had been and what I had been doing that day and night.

"I had lied so many times that at that point, I didn't know who I had told what. I still tried lying a little, but then I started crying and really broke down. It occurred to me then that I never thought I would ever do heroin and that I had always told myself that would never be me—but it was. I knew I hated my life and that I was sucked in so deep that I had no idea what to do but to get high for the rest of my life.

"My mother and those counselors were so loving, and they just kept telling me that I could be happy again without using drugs and that I was loved for who I am. I just needed to hear that was possible.

"Today, I'm so grateful to the person who knew what happened to me that night and told people who might be in a position to help. If no one had told anyone, I don't know where I would be right now."

If at all possible, both parents should attend the first appointment with their child. *Working together*, they can wear down resistance better than one parent alone. Their teamwork also sends a strong message to the adolescent about the importance of this issue. Teenagers frequently say something like, "My mom cares, but my dad doesn't care if I smoke pot." These young people are often quite surprised to hear that dad really does care after all.

Finally, if it is very difficult to get a teen to treatment, parents can go to the first few sessions themselves. The sessions can focus on beginning the family recovery process and how to encourage the adolescent to begin as well. Research has shown that these parent-only meetings can facilitate getting the adolescent into treatment eventually.[6]

Adolescents with a substance use disorder should receive specific substance treatment. In the early 2000s, an important researcher in the field of adolescent addictions, Dr. Paula Riggs, a professor of psychiatry at the University of Colorado, conducted a study in which she randomized adolescents with co-occurring attention deficit hyperactivity disorder (ADHD) and substance use disorder to either medicine or placebo for ADHD.[7] The adolescents did not receive any therapy for their substance use disorder. The results showed the medicine successfully treated ADHD but did nothing for the substance use disorder.

What Dr. Riggs's findings underscored is that when there are two problems—substance abuse and co-occurring ADHD, anxiety, depression, or some other psychiatric problem—both problems need to be addressed. Substance use disorder does not magically disappear because an adolescent's other problems are being treated. The substance abuse or addiction must be addressed too.

Adolescents who have a substance use disorder and a co-occurring psychiatric disorder should have concurrent treatment of these problems. Years ago, people believed it impossible to diagnose or treat co-occurring psychiatric problems in someone who was using substances. Nowadays we know how to tease out these different problems with a careful timeline assessment of the adolescent's life.[8] Current research shows that 80 percent of adolescents in substance treatment have a co-occurring psychiatric disorder[9]—and that fewer than 25 percent of adolescents in substance treatment receive care for both psychiatric and substance problems.[10] This lack of integrated mental health–substance treatment not only causes needless suffering but also leads to poorer treatment outcomes.[11,12] After all, it's hard enough to overcome an addiction, much less overcome it while in the middle of a major depressive episode. A comprehensive assessment is crucial because it guides the rest of treatment. This is also why in Dr. Thurstone's practice, families often meet jointly with their therapist and child psychiatrist in the first session: a comprehensive treatment can immediately follow a comprehensive assessment.

PARENTS WHO HAVE BEEN THERE

"I knew my son had a drug problem, but I strongly suspected something else was going on with him," said Lisa Taylor, the Colorado Springs mother whose son continues to struggle with addiction. "I wasn't surprised when he was also diagnosed with attention deficit disorder (ADD), but you could have knocked me over when the therapist just looked at me and said, 'It appears to have something to do with you, actually.'

"For years, I have dealt with serious illness. I have multiple sclerosis, and I have been treated for leukemia. I have had related surgeries, and my children have seen me when I have been very sick.

"I also divorced my son's father and remarried.

"What I eventually pieced together is that my son was deeply worried about what would happen to him if something happened to me. He didn't know where he'd go. He'd also started to question why a loving God would allow his mom to continue to be so sick.

"He desperately needed treatment for much more than addiction."

Adolescents should receive treatment in the least restrictive setting necessary. In substance treatment, there are different levels of care. Level 1 includes regular outpatient care during which adolescents and their families have one to two appointments each week. Level 2 is intensive outpatient care, and adolescents typically have appointments about three to five times each week. Level 3 treatment is residential, and that's when adolescents stay overnight in a facility for several weeks to months. In general, it is best to pursue the lowest level of care that is safe, because it gives adolescents and their families a chance to make changes in their usual environment as treatment progresses. For example, therapists and families might have the opportunity to work together to alter the adolescent's peer group or to get involved in positive activities that promote long-term sobriety.

However, there are times when adolescents are out of control, not safe to themselves or others, or have failed less restrictive treatments. In these special situations, a level 2 program (intensive outpatient) or level 3 program (residential treatment) might be needed.

Medications may sometimes help treat either the substance use disorder or the co-occurring psychiatric disorder. As already mentioned, co-occurring psychiatric disorders are a poor prognostic indicator for adolescent substance treatment outcomes. Sometimes medications can help treat these co-occurring psychiatric problems and improve overall treatment outcomes. For example, while mild depression typically responds well to therapy alone, moderate to severe depression is usually an indication for an antidepressant.

Medications that, to date, have been studied in adolescents for co-occurring psychiatric and substance use disorders include atomoxetine for ADHD,[13] fluoxetine for depression,[14] and OROS methylphenidate for ADHD.[15] All of these medications were generally safe in nonabstinent adolescents *who were seen at least weekly for substance treatment.* Fluoxetine was also found to be better than placebo for depression.[16] OROS methylphenidate was better than placebo on some, but not all, measures of ADHD and substance treatment outcome.[17]

Several medications are used to treat addiction directly. Among them:

Buprenorphine/naloxone is a medication that has an indication from the U.S. Food and Drug Administration for the treatment of opioid-use disorder in people sixteen and older. This medication might be indicated for an adolescent who has physical dependence on opioids, such a prescription pain pills or heroin, and has not been able to stop using with or without treatment. Buprenorphine/naloxone reduces cravings for opiates and reduces withdrawal symptoms. It does this by binding to the same brain receptors as heroin and other opioids—but without producing a high. So the use of this drug isn't really substituting one addiction for another. On the contrary, research shows that when prescribed and monitored appropriately, buprenorphine/naloxone can safely improve treatment outcomes for youth with addiction to opioids.[18] However, because some research shows buprenorphine may alter brain development in the long run, it is wise to have a plan for tapering this medication eventually.[19]

One school of thought is that people with opioid dependence should be allowed to suffer through substance withdrawal without medical intervention. The thinking goes that people who experience withdrawal will be less likely to relapse and become dependent on the drug again. However, these claims are unfounded. As already mentioned, research shows otherwise: outcomes are improved with appropriate medical treatment during withdrawal. We would not withhold available treatment to reduce suffering associated with other medical conditions—and we should not do so when treating addiction either.

N-acetylcysteine (administered at 1200 milligrams twice daily) is another medicine that decreased some measures of marijuana use in a study of older adolescents and young adults.[20] This medication is available over the counter and has very few known side effects. As always, consult your health-care professional before starting this medication.

These are the only medications that directly treat addiction and have been studied in adolescents.

Other medications that might be used off-label include acamprosate, disulfiram, and naltrexone for alcohol use disorders. Acamprosate and naltrexone may decrease cravings for alcohol and can be used in combination.

Naltrexone also blocks the effects of heroin and prescription pain pills. If monitored by a third party, it may be helpful in certain situations. It is also available in a monthly injection form, called Vivitrol. The injectable form may be easier to monitor than a daily pill. Getting a health insurance provider to cover this medication can be tricky. So if you and your health-care provider think this is a good option, you should call your health insurance provider yourself to investigate benefits and start making the case for this treatment option.

Disulfiram makes people nauseous and quite sick if they drink alcohol. To be effective, it typically needs to be administered by an outside source, such as parents or a treatment program. If not monitored, patients tend to stop taking the medication.

It is important to understand the following about medications that may be used to treat adolescent substance use disorder:

- They can be helpful—and that they can be helpful to treatment underscores the need for a comprehensive assessment with a qualified clinician as outlined above.
- Their use does not mean the "exchange of one addiction for another." A lot of parents understandably want their children to be off substances entirely. While it is wise to be conservative and judicious with medications, especially for minors, there is a time and place for their use. There are also very big differences between using alcohol, marijuana, or heroin and taking a prescription antidepressant.

- Medications should not be the backbone of adolescent substance treatment. Instead the core of treatment is good psychotherapy. Medications should be used only to augment psychotherapy—and it is tough to underscore the importance of this enough. People struggling with substance use disorders need far more than "med checks." Think carefully about whether a clinician is focusing more on medication management than on addressing co-occurring mental health problems and underlying life skills, such as copying with cravings, communication, and anger management. Avoid engaging or working with a clinician who appears to want to solve all issues with pharmaceuticals.

- Treatment should be empathetic, motivational, and nonjudgmental. Old-school treatments stressed the importance of confrontation until someone admitted they were an addict. These approaches to treatment made adolescents' problems worse.[21] More recent research shows that a treatment called motivational interviewing, which stresses the importance of being empathetic and nonjudgmental, is effective for adolescents[22] because it can help them elicit and understand their own internal reasons for wanting to change. The therapist joins with these motivations and then gently helps adolescents see how substance use ultimately does not help accomplish their objectives. For example, if teenagers want to do well in school, the therapist may help them understand how substance use will stand in the way. So look for providers who are affirming, warm, friendly, and nonjudgmental and who appear to understand your teen—all without conveying any support of substance use. Guard against therapists who communicate approval of substance use when trying to relate to their young patients.

Finally, many substance treatment providers are in recovery themselves, and there are several myths regarding the importance and relevance of their personal experiences to the treatment of addiction and the process of entering recovery. On the one hand, therapists in recovery can offer the advantages of personal experience, and it can be very helpful to have peers and mentors who have faced similar situations. But on the other hand, we don't require our oncologist to have had cancer or our orthopedist to have had a broken ankle to treat us. There is just no scientific evidence that substance treatment providers in recovery produce better outcomes than those who are not. There are well-meaning therapists in recovery who talk too much about their own experiences without listening to a family's unique story, and who think their method of recovery is the only way anyone should go about achieving sobriety. Then there is Julia Timmerman, one of the most skillful adolescent substance treatment providers in Denver, Colorado, if not the United States. She grew up a Seventh-Day Adventist and has never used alcohol or drugs in her life.

On a similar note, it is unnecessary to match therapists by age, gender, race, ethnicity, or other demographic variables. While patients may sometimes have preferences, research does not support the need to seek out a therapist based on any of these variables alone.

So the bottom line is this: a good therapist is a good therapist regardless of his or her past experience of personal recovery, age, gender, race, ethnicity, or other baseline variable.

DISCUSSION QUESTIONS

- *How can you be more empathetic, motivational, and nonjudgmental?*
- *If you had to identify a substance treatment provider for anyone in your family, could you do so today? If not, what is your plan for finding one?*
- *What are some of the specific things you have noticed to make you think your child may need substance treatment?*
- *What does the ideal treatment program look like to you? What would it look like to your teen?*

5

SPECIFIC FAMILY OBJECTIVES DURING TREATMENT

The Theory

Because families have much influence on a teen's decision to use substances, they should be involved in treatment.

Before getting to the scientific principles, let's cover common sense related to family therapy.

First, parents do not need to be perfect but good enough. Make this your mantra. Say it over and over and early and often. Parents cannot provide all of the protective factors we'll cover later in this chapter to their children at all times. Accepting this reality is freeing and alleviates a great deal of the fear and guilt that drive parents to be too hard on themselves and others.

Second, patience is a virtue—and a must. Families often try to make positive changes without success and prematurely conclude the recommendations and therapy didn't work—and won't work. That's a lot like a soccer player saying, "I kicked the ball and didn't score a goal, so kicking the ball doesn't work." Putting these principles into place takes practice, so try to remain positive until you get them right. As with many things, practice will, indeed, help ensure success.

Third, what is good for parents is usually good for children. Parents with high self-esteem are often good—make that great—for their kids. But when they arrive in therapy, parents are often struggling with a lot of the same issues as their children. They are not in a position emotionally or psychologically to be of help to the very young person they desperately wish to save. They are embarrassed and worried about what others are thinking of the situation that has landed their family in therapy. They feel inadequate and like a failure—and so they're often very hard on themselves and others. Their fear is paralyzing.

So another important goal of family therapy is to help parents raise their self-esteem too. They need to like themselves because they're confident about their parenting and utterly convinced they're acting in their child's best interest. They need to move into a healthy enough place to recognize that their child's bad decision making is not a reflection of their value and effectiveness as parents or as people.

Confident parents, in turn, can help instill confidence in their children. Raising a child with a healthy sense of self-esteem—or confidence in his or her worth—is a powerful protectant from drug abuse. Teenagers are sometimes down on themselves as they learn to navigate the world, but when they have a solid sense of self-respect and like their natural selves, chemically induced good times often aren't as alluring.

Family sessions frequently focus on what members can do specifically to be helpful and encourage sobriety. In technical terms, these actions are referred to as "protective or resiliency factors."[1] They're detailed in this chapter to help parents understand the main goals of family therapy—one of which is to build up the self-esteem of the child who is struggling with addiction.

PARENTS WHO HAVE BEEN THERE

"I grew up under an authoritarian roof, and my husband grew up under a neglectful one," said Jo McGuire, a Colorado Springs drug-testing expert. "We thought together we balanced out, but it was a big mistake for us to view our collective approach to parenting as somehow 'blended.' Instead, we needed to be individuals, yes, but more like a team where the members are cross-trained so that when one person falls down, the other can step in to execute seamlessly in that role. We needed to be in agreement with one game plan.

"Now, in hindsight, I see what a mess my husband and I were: I was always the one saying something, and he rarely did. I was always perceived as the disciplinarian and party-pooper, and he got to be the fun guy.

"Looking back, I thought I was in control and knew all of the important things I needed to about my kids, but I realize now that I was way more of an enabler than I ever would have believed then. That's because I was just so tired of being the bad guy all the time—and my kids picked up on that. They finally told me one day that they knew when they were younger that they could always get me to say yes to whatever they wanted. All they had to do was figure out my parameters—so, if they could convince me of X and agree to Y, I would always permit the Z I had rejected in the first place.

"So here you always are, thinking you've made a good decision—that you even compromised well with your child—but you actually gave in to something that contributed to their downfall. And that's one of the big things about addiction: when you're dealing with a child who has this problem, the manipulation is ever-exhausting, and most of us are just not mentally prepared to deal with it. When parents aren't working together or trying to be more in sync, it's even more difficult to handle."

Now let's take a look at specific principles that science shows us are helpful ingredients for family therapy.

BE CARING, EMPATHETIC, AND EMOTIONALLY RESPONSIVE[2]

Even when adolescents act as if they don't care about any adults, they thrive on having at least one who cares for them. Parents can demonstrate the caring their adolescent craves by listening, understanding, and responding appropriately to their needs. Too often, parents express their care and concern by talking, lecturing, and planning agendas for their child. Remember to pay attention to the child's behaviors, interests, and words—and then take the extra step to convey you're paying attention, because what often seems like no big deal to an adult can be a very big deal to the adolescent.

Do not make the mistake of thinking that validating a person's feelings means you must agree with him or her. And don't dismiss your teen's feelings by trying to fix them right away or by being too quick to offer advice. Acknowledge the pain your child is experiencing, and empathize.

BE AN AUTHORITATIVE PARENT[3,4]

Parents should know the differences among authoritative, authoritarian, passive, and neglectful parenting styles.

Authoritative parents are the most effective at preventing substance abuse and other problem behaviors. These parents combine warmth and understanding with the firm boundaries that children need to grow up healthy. They model effective communication, problem solving, and anger management—which are very important because children learn many of their most important social skills by observing their parents.[5]

Authoritative parents are both demanding and responsive. In the demanding column, these parents require their children to follow the house rules through discipline, supervision, and willingness to confront a teenager who is breaking the rules. In the responsive column, these parents understand and take care of their child's wishes and needs by being accepting, affectionate, communicative, intimate, and loving. Authoritative parents spend time with their teens, listen to what's on their mind, and take steps to be helpful. They reward good behavior and calmly discuss misbehavior.

Unfortunately, parents often fall into the traps of being too authoritarian, passive, or neglectful.

- Authoritarian parents. These parents are demanding but unresponsive to their teenager's feelings, needs, and desires. They sometimes use name-calling, nagging, scolding threats, yelling, or physical punishment. They dictate to their children, frequently communicating, "It's my way or the highway."
- Passive parents. These parents are responsive to and affectionate toward their children, but they have trouble demanding much, if anything, of them. They frequently let their children do whatever they want—and then move quickly to clean up behind the messes their kids have made to shield them from the natural consequences of their decisions.

- Neglectful parents. These parents are neither demanding nor responsive. They withdraw from a situation and withhold both affection and discipline. Often, neglectful parents are overwhelmed by their own feelings of guilt and anger at the situation, so they shut down and shut out others. When a child gets a failing grade, a neglectful parent might ignore it entirely. A passive parent might express disapproval—and then agree to let the child go to the movies anyway. An authoritarian parent might say, "That better be at least a B next semester, or else!"—and then proceed to ground the child for a couple of weeks. The authoritative parent is firm and, at the same time, understanding. He or she might say, "Tell me what happened with this grade. I want you to grow up to be successful. What can I do to help you improve this grade?"

THE TREATMENT PROVIDER'S PERSPECTIVE

"It's important for parents to recognize how their issues, not their child's issues, but their issues, affect their parenting style," said Frank Szachta, director of the Cornerstone Program in Centennial, Colorado. A self-described "Big Book Thumper," he is a certified addictions counselor whose long hair, easy laugh, and intentionally salty language aimed at just the right moment and just the right kid win a lot of irreverent and rebellious teen hearts and minds.

"Frequently, parents walk in with a great deal of baggage that's about fear and guilt," he said. "That fear and guilt have a domino effect that informs everything they do or don't do. Because of these feelings, one parent overreacts and says, 'I have been too permissive. I need to clamp down. I have given my child too much freedom.' Another says, 'I am too hard and harsh, so now I need to say yes to everything because if I'm nicer, my daughter will like me again.'

"All of these premises are false, and because they're coming from fear and guilt, they push people into these extreme parenting styles and all of the negative thoughts and feelings that go with them. Soon parenting styles clash with one controlling the situation and the other enabling it. When we add a divorced couple to the mix, the dynamics are more complex because divorce adds stress to parent decision making. All of this is why parents can wind up so far afield.

"We want parents to work from a place of unity, love, and logic instead. We usually begin this process by helping parents understand the three Cs: you didn't cause it, you can't control it, and you can't cure it. This understanding helps alleviate parents' guilt or fear that they caused this problem and are doing the 'wrong' things to address it. Getting to this point is why seeing an individual, objective third party to hash out all of these issues with is so important."

Parents must, of course, consider child discipline. It is one of their most important roles as parents. Basic behavioral principles show there are at least four main ways to shape behavior.[6] Here are the four main approaches—and how they may apply to your household. Note that the authoritative parent uses a combination of these techniques:

First, there is positive reinforcement. This means your child gets something good in exchange for his or her behavior. Examples of this include verbal praise, such as a "nice job," or a privilege, such as getting to go to a concert or an extra hour of time with friends. So make sure you "catch" your child being good and reward them appropriately. Be specific to the task, too, and praise effort as much as success.

Second, there is positive punishment. The most common example of this is getting scolded because of misbehavior. For example, a parent says "I'm very disappointed" when his or her child is caught in a lie. While positive punishment clearly has its time and place, authoritarian parents tend to rely on this method too much.

Third is negative punishment. This is what happens when your child loses something considered "good" because he or she has misbehaved. Examples include grounding a teenager and the loss of cell phone, car, social media, or Internet privileges.

Finally, there is negative reinforcement. This happens when a teenager gets to do away with something "bad." Examples of this approach include getting a reprieve from doing the dishes or from a curfew in exchange for good behavior. Of note, the term *negative reinforcement* is commonly used incorrectly to refer to rewarding bad behavior by paying attention to it. However, in scientifically precise language, that is actually positive reinforcement because children are getting something they want in exchange for their behavior. These terms can be confusing, so it's a good idea to ask questions of knowledgeable people to help you determine how to apply these concepts to your family.

Parents shouldn't lose sight of how teens also use these principles, even if inadvertently. For example, if your teenagers are super nice to you, they may be using positive reinforcement to get what they want. If they yell at you to get you to give in, they may be inflicting positive punishment. If they give you the cold shoulder and withhold their attention and affection, they may be trying to inflict negative punishment. Finally, if your teenager does extra chores that you normally do, he or she might be using negative reinforcement to get something from you.

Not all of these things are necessarily bad. They're simply how humans are motivated. Regardless, it is helpful for parents to have a grasp of these principles so they know how to influence their child's behavior—and how their child may be influencing their parenting.

"Children need to face discipline and consequences, but parents often get them mixed up in ways that break down the parent-child relationship and send very confusing messages that can result in bigger problems," said Father John Bonavitacola, whose Catholic parish in Arizona operates a grade school.

"Let's take a boy I know, for example. When he was in the first grade, he wasn't doing well on spelling tests, and his parents were frustrated. One week, there was a father-son campout, and the boy was very excited to go. His parents told him he couldn't attend if he didn't do well on his spelling test. So the boy studied really hard. His parents called out all of the words to him, and it was clear he knew how to spell them. But during the test, a teacher caught him cheating. It turns out he was so scared that he was going to miss out on something really good—in this case, that campout—that he didn't trust himself and did something really bad.

"So I try to help parents understand a couple of important concepts. The first is that they should tie the consequences of behavior to appropriate things. In the case of that boy, a failed spelling test should have been addressed within the context of school, not with denying him the opportunity to spend time with his father, which is something very good for them both. Spending time with a parent should have nothing to do with a spelling test. Young people ask what one has to do with the other, and they think things like this are illogical—and they're right. What lesson do children typically learn when they're confused like this? They've learned that they can't please their parents no matter what they do.

"The second thing I focus on is helping parents build a team or a community of trusted people who can help them discipline their children. Parents do not need to be the enforcer all of the time. They should find teachers, pastors, and coaches they trust and take themselves out of the middle of every difficult situation. The more parents can enroll a third party to give the consequences, the better. So if the child gets in trouble at school, let the school handle it. There is no need for parents to impose still more consequences, which will, once again, make them the bad guy. Parents just need to communicate that they didn't make up the consequences and that they cannot interfere with them. 'Wow, that principal is tough. Bummer.' or 'Man, that teacher is rigid. Who knew?' or 'That cop gave you a curfew ticket? Sorry.'

"It is fine for parents to remind their children of what could happen to them, but engaging in constant battles and shielding your kids from the aftermath of their poor choices is very unwise."

MAINTAIN BEHAVIORAL CONTROL, NOT PSYCHOLOGICAL CONTROL[7]

Behavioral control refers to being demanding as described above—meaning parents establish and communicate clear rules they enforce consistently. Parents with good behavioral control track their child's activities; monitor friends, grades, homework, school attendance, and whereabouts; and use both rewards (such as verbal praise and privileges) and punishment.

The common mistake parents make is to try to assume psychological control of their child. That's when they intrude into the emotional state of their child or try to "get in his head." They frequently interrupt their children with interjections aimed at changing their feelings ("That's silly. You should . . . "). They often use guilt ("Don't you care about what you're doing to our family?"). They also withhold love and emotions or become overly protective and involved in their children's lives. When a parent is overinvolved, children often lose healthy autonomy. They can become so dependent that their parents become enablers of continued substance use by protecting their children from some of the natural consequences of their drug use.

Parents need to decide the most appropriate balance between protection and autonomy for their child—all the while keeping in mind that protection is not always beneficial. This is also a tough balancing act made all the more difficult because it's hard for anyone to objectively assess their own behavior. This is another reason it's a good idea for parents to seek more objective assessments from a support group or qualified clinician. They should be open to feedback and coachable when it comes from a trusted source.

THE TREATMENT PROVIDER'S PERSPECTIVE

"Let's not forget that we're dealing with teenagers here," said Frank Szachta, whose Cornerstone Program regularly hosts "sober-social" events for hundreds of young people in recovery. "They are discovering autonomy—and they should be. That's why we describe them as naturally rebellious. They are trying to separate from their parents. This is normal. In this context, not telling mom and dad the details about your latest girlfriend has been extended to not telling them about your substance use. Withholding information about getting high adds to the teenager's sense of autonomy.

"So here's what happens, and it's very important for parents to understand: the substance-addicted kid is thinking, 'Getting sober is acquiescing to the control of my parents. They just want me to bend to their wishes.'

"This teenager has to find a way to own his recovery. He has to see it as his and not as an extension of whatever it is his parents want him to do. And if there's a way to help retain his natural and normal sense of rebellion within sobriety? Great! Let your young person in recovery have the freedom to push boundaries, because that's what teenagers normally want to do.

"I see it all the time," Szachta added with a chuckle. "The new kids come in and connect with older kids in the program who take them under their wings and invite them to hang out, listen to loud music, dance, and stay up too late—which is all completely normal for teenagers to want to do. Our program is very much the teenagers' program, and it is just fine with me if the young people in it begin to see it as an expression of rebellion against their parents. I'm fine with providing the place that lets them continue to push the boundaries of going off on their own and doing their own thing. They're sober, and they're doing what comes naturally to them, which is feeding their insatiable desire to have fun.

"What's really cool is when parents trust and get to say yes to their kid again. They get to say yes to the lock-ins and the dances and to the sleepovers at another sober kid's house. And you know what they tell me? 'That's the best sleep I have had in years.'"

MAINTAIN SELF-CARE, BOUNDARIES, AND COPARENTING.[8,9]

Having a spouse or partner in whom you can confide helps to improve parenting. If you're married or in a committed partnership, it is very important to take care of that relationship. Parents frequently focus all of their energy on their struggling teen at the expense of their intimacy with each other. This often leads to resentment, discord—and poor parenting.

Another valuable concept from Al-Anon deserves a mention here. It's called detachment, and it involves lovingly creating a distance between yourself and a loved one's addiction. This means life goes on despite the addiction, and it doesn't center on the addiction. Couples should pursue their hobbies. They should go out to dinner and discuss things other than their children. They should spend time with their friends.

Detachment is vitally important to the protection of relationships. Couples who can't focus on anything other than their hurting child often burn out. They become very angry with their child—sometimes blaming him or her for the ruination of marriage and family. They can become so angry with their child that they're drained of the emotional resources they need to actually help their son or daughter.

In the same sense that parents must establish healthy boundaries to keep a child's addiction from encroaching, they must also recognize that there are things about their lives they should not impose on their children. Teenagers are not responsible for adult issues, such as marital dynamics and their parents' finances. They are not responsible for problems parents experience at work or problems parents have socially. It is important for parents to work out these issues without involving their children.

Finally, parents, whether married or divorced, should work diligently to parent their children together. Their ability to agree on general issues is very important to the treatment of adolescents with substance use disorder and related problems. When parents have obviously different opinions about how to handle their teen's substance use, their teen frequently pits them against each other, all the while justifying his or her drug use. Parents should do their best to work together calmly to present a clear, consistent, and firmly unified front to their child. To do so, they must empathize with each other rather than fight for their points of view to be heard.

THE TREATMENT PROVIDER'S PERSPECTIVE

"The first casualty of a substance abuse problem in a family is a sense of humor," said Frank Szachta. "In treatment, it's just as important to get parents laughing again. That's self-care. We say all the time, 'Don't take yourself too seriously,' but let's face it: there is nothing more serious than your child's life being threatened. So it's a very big deal when parents can achieve the detachment that gives them the ability to take things lightly and laugh again. What is profound is seeing parents laugh again even when their kids are not successful in sobriety."

SPEND TIME TOGETHER[10]

Spending time together as a family and having fun family activities develops closeness. It also provides opportunities for understanding and teachable moments. Ideally, families have rituals and traditions, such as special meals, movie nights, holiday/birthday celebrations, and vacations that promote both time together and family organization and order.[11] Try to avoid discussion about substances and other family problems.

And if your adolescent-in-treatment doesn't seem to want to spend time with you? That's normal. In this case, start low and go slow, but go.

THE TREATMENT PROVIDER'S PERSPECTIVE

"Remember that teenagers—especially substance-abusing teens in the early stages of recovery—are not dying to spend more time with their parents," said Frank Szachta. "If they are, I am concerned, because that means they're trying to manipulate them. They're like Eddie Haskell from *Leave It to Beaver*. 'Hiiiiii, Mother. I am so very pleased to spend time with you this evening.' Sorry, but that's just not a normal teenage statement. Usually they want to be out from under you and with their friends.

"So the time we're talking about here is qualitative, not quantitative. It is not quality time if it communicates, 'I'm controlling you,' or if everyone's sitting through gritted teeth and folded arms to watch television.

"The idea here is not that your kid needs to spend countless hours with your family, but that when you are all together, there's not that sense of distrust or walking around on eggshells. Frankly, when you can trust your kid again, you won't mind that you don't see him as much—which is why it's really important for everyone to be in treatment to develop that trust again.

"When teens are in recovery, their sense of alienation begins to dissipate. Sure, they're still out late, but keeping a vampire's schedule is just what they do. In time, they come around again because they know the time you do spend together is enjoyable for all concerned. Getting there is a lot of work, and it's difficult, but it really can happen."

BE A HEALTHY ROLE MODEL[12]

In his talks with parents, Indiana State Supreme Court Justice Steven David sums it up this way: "If your child grows up seeing that you are not able to watch a ballgame or socialize with anyone without a drink in your hand, it will probably be learned behavior on their part—and they may be such good learners that they start emulating your behavior early."

It is true that teens learn many of their coping and social skills through what they see around them. By serving as role models, parents have an opportunity to teach their children how to communicate effectively, deal with stress, handle anger, live a balanced life, manage money, and abstain from substance use.

Yes, abstaining from alcohol and drug use prevents children from using substances themselves. For example, teens of parents who drink even occasionally are twice as likely to have trouble with binge drinking as their peers who have parents who do not drink.[13] Similarly, teens of parents who used marijuana in the last year are twice as likely to have past-year marijuana use as are teens of parents who never used the drug.[14]

These studies do not prove a causal link between parental substance use and adolescent substance use. However, they raise concerns about the possible impact of parental substance use behaviors. Adolescents frequently get their first taste of alcohol or tobacco by pilfering from their parents' supply. Seeing their parents use may give adolescents a more favorable impression of substances.

If parents want to prevent substance use in their children, the safest strategy is for them to abstain from using substances. Abstinence is also one of the most helpful ways to assist a child who is in substance treatment.

If parents choose not to abstain from substance use, they should certainly avoid storing any substances in the home, or they should keep substances locked up. Parents also should not involve their children in substance-using behavior, such as fetching a beer from the refrigerator or ferrying a pack of cigarettes from another room. Another strategy could be to have only single servings of alcohol in the house. That way teens are not able to siphon off liquor and replace it with water.

THE TREATMENT PROVIDER'S PERSPECTIVE

"I have known many parents who have quit imbibing as a statement of solidarity with their child in substance treatment—who they say is one of the most important people in the world to them," said Frank Szachta. "These are people who are putting their lives where their mouths are.

"When parents say they will not, or cannot, remove alcohol—or any other substance—from their home when a young person in treatment is living there, perhaps they should stop to consider their own relationship with that substance.

"I'm not saying you shouldn't drink," he continued. "I'm saying it does not need to be in your house. Yes, your child can get this substance anywhere, but your home needs to be a safe place, a sanctuary, for your substance-abusing child. Teenagers do not have control of their homes, but we adults do, and it is our job as parents to protect them, not lay traps and minefields."

TEACH GENERAL LIFE SKILLS[15]

During treatment, clinicians teach and practice various skills with teenagers. These include anger management, goal setting, communication, educational/vocational skills, mood regulation, and problem solving. During family sessions, the skills are reviewed again so parents can model and teach them at home. We will discuss some of these life skills in more detail in the next chapter.

COMMUNICATE CLEAR EXPECTATIONS ABOUT SUBSTANCE USE[16]

Children of parents who clearly communicate that substance use is not acceptable are less likely to use than if their parents present a mixed message. This sounds like common sense, but frequently youth believe their parents think substance use is no big deal. They then use this perception to justify ongoing use.

Parents who host parties for teens where drugs and alcohol are consumed—they're called "social hosts"—send highly mixed messages and are often acting in violation of law. Their common justification is, "At least they're using in a safe environment." However, social hosting is based on the false assumption that kids are going to use substances no matter what, an assumption that has not been supported by science.[17]

Head back to chapter 1 for a refresher on how the developing brain works and is especially vulnerable to substance addiction. Introducing young people to substances while they are in this crucial phase of brain development—of which so much has been learned in only the last five years—is doing them no favors.

THE TREATMENT PROVIDER'S PERSPECTIVE

"Okay, so here's a really good analogy for you," said Frank Szachta, using his hand to mimic a pistol. "You've got six shots in your gun. Just six—and that's all you get. These shots represent the things that are absolutely unacceptable to you, and you better use them sparingly because these are all you have. They're also designed to communicate serious business: no one should ever fire a bullet without heavy consideration first, and everyone should know that you're packing this heat. If you think you're just going to reload, well, then, now you've become a tyrant—and chances are really good that you're acting out of fear, and no one is going to respect your idea of the law, or the absolutes you said you would not tolerate.

"Now, let's say you and your pistol are in your house, where you've obviously put up walls. The walls represent all of the boundaries and limits you've established to protect your child and everyone else living in your house. They represent your values, and they also make clear your limits of acceptability, whether we're talking about morality, legality, or general social behavior. They establish that your kid's self-destructive behavior will not be tolerated in the most important place in his or her life, which is the one place in all the world where he or she is loved unconditionally. These walls are always 'home' to your child.

"Your walls are marked, everyone knows where they are, and they provide the safe haven and shelter your children need in a world where walls are increasingly torn down at faster and faster rates, and kids without walls at home are left lost and searching.

"Your walls are immovable, but that doesn't mean your kid isn't going to try to climb over them, navigate around them, and otherwise ignore them. They are testing and challenging your limits. That is normal—and all of their efforts, however annoying, are just fine because you're a staunch member of your kid's team, you're watching carefully, granting privileges when earned and refusing to accept their unacceptable behavior.

"But there's still a lot going on inside those walls of yours. Your daughter is wearing berets at the dinner table every night and lecturing the rest of you about her radical politics. She has become a vegetarian, knowing very well that you love a great steak every week, and she is pushing to go to a university you have absolutely no intention of giving a dime to. Meanwhile, your son is refusing to go to church, recently pierced his tongue without discussing the matter with you first, and he can't seem to pull up any of his grades higher than a C average.

"Boy, have you got some decisions to make. Do you fire a shot? Are these things really worth that firepower?

"You are, after all, free to continue pointing out the walls in your home, so maybe that shot—which you have only six of—isn't worth firing.

"Don't tell your daughter she can't believe in a particular ideology. Just explain that you'd rather not discuss these matters with her around the dinner table because you would like to digest your steak in peace— and you're happy to explain why you think her views are off-track over a good plate of quinoa. And sure, feel free to let your son know that you think his pierced tongue was a dumb move because it may not blow over well with potential employers, but that you would be pleased to take him to the mall because you think that smart-alecky T-shirt he has been wanting would actually look nice on him.

"What your kids have done is what normal kids do: they are producing tension around your walls. A lot of parents make the mistake of thinking that confrontations like these can and should be avoided. A lot of parents of drug-using teens look back and realize that they didn't set up walls because they wanted to be liked and to avoid the messiness and difficulty of enforcing critical boundaries. They harbor enormous guilt for ignoring the warning signs of drug addiction.

"Continued drug use is when a lot of smart parents decide to start firing their shots. They have communicated that drug use is unacceptable and could result in serious consequences that might even mean the young person has to move out. So the choice is put in your young person's hands, and he knows what the consequences are and will have to face them."

REQUIRE TEENS TO CONTRIBUTE TO HOUSEHOLD FUNCTIONING[18]

Teens who contribute to their households in meaningful and valuable ways often feel like important and valued members of their family— which builds their self-esteem. Work together to determine household chores, financial payments, or other contributions that help an adolescent feel appreciated. Involving youth in these activities also alleviates parents of a lot of stress and resentment they often feel.

And as tough as it might be, try to recognize that a messy room may not be the first place to focus when dealing with a teenager in substance treatment or early recovery. If your son or daughter were receiving chemotherapy, you probably wouldn't be too hung up on whether he or she made the bed that morning.

COUNT ON EXTENDED FAMILY [19]

A healthy social network can provide positive role models and support to help youth stay clean. Families can help provide these types of relationships.

HELP YOUTH HAVE MEANING AND PURPOSE [20]

Research shows that youth who have long-range goals and plans to achieve them are less likely to use substances. Families can help their teenagers set goals and determine the steps required to reach them. If this is a big struggle, start very small and celebrate every success.

And as hurtful as this may be, a lot of parents might find that they are not the best people to help their drug-abusing child make initial steps toward establishing these goals and plans. It is often a good idea to find someone else—maybe a long-haired, foul-mouthed, music-loving counselor like Frank Szachta, or a clean-cut military officer who plays competitive tennis like Dr. Thurstone—to provide this guidance and support.

In summary, parents have many tools to handle the situation of teen drug use. All these basic tools start with a warm, caring relationship. In the next chapter, we discuss how to put this theory to practice

DISCUSSION QUESTIONS

- *What is your parenting style, and is it in conflict with another? If so, how?*
- *Which of the principles of how parents positively influence their child's behavior seems most relevant to you and why?*
- *What are your home's walls? What are the nonnegotiables that guarantee you'll fire one of your six shots?*
- *What are some of the ways your family can start working to promote these principles at home?*

6

SPECIFIC FAMILY OBJECTIVES DURING SESSION

The Practice

So what should families discuss during substance treatment anyway? Good therapy sessions build on the theories outlined in chapter 5. In this chapter, we discuss three strategies that many families find helpful: goal setting, effective communication, and effective problem solving. There are many other helpful skills to learn and develop, but these three are basic and fundamentally important to long-term success.

There are a lot of different ways to help people acquire these skills, and programs approach this guidance differently. Some programs don't even offer family therapy, instead opting to provide separate twelve-step support groups for youth in recovery and support groups for parents of kids struggling with substance use disorders. That might work for your family. Or a support group might be beneficial in combination with regularly scheduled family sessions. Or perhaps you're at a stage where you think it's best to focus on family therapy and connect with a support group at a later time in the not-so-distant future.

Family therapy recognizes that every family is profoundly different. Families have unique structures and patterns of communication, and all members are affected by these powerful dynamics shaping their lives and their abilities to interact with others to form families of their own. Because family members are so deeply intertwined, illness in one member might indicate a larger problem with the unit that, if left unaddressed, could harm other members too. Models of family therapy generally aim to strengthen the entire unit through the encouragement and strengthening of individual members.

This overarching goal is especially important when one member is struggling with addiction—a condition that affects everyone in a household. To address the problem as successfully as possible, families benefit from working with neutral, third-party therapists who can help them have unique insight into how their own unit functions and develop strategies for addressing conflicts, anxieties, and changes differently.

During therapy sessions, families are often challenged to take responsibility for certain problems and to use their collective and individual strengths to help their family unit function in a loving, healthy, and productive manner.

PARENTS WHO HAVE BEEN THERE

"It is hard to describe how consuming and exhausting it is to care for a child who has this kind of problem," said Rino S., a father of three from Arvada, Colorado, who, along with his wife, Starr, has worked diligently to address one daughter's substance addiction and eating disorder. "When someone recommended that we go through family therapy, I remember thinking it was just going to be one more thing that would deplete my limited human resources—but the counselor was very good. I saw a lot of good things come from just being given the opportunity to sit down as a family. That was really helpful. Without a doubt, everything has focused on our one daughter, and the other two kids have unfairly come in second too much. That is, at least, obvious to everyone now. My wife and I are much smarter about how not to overlook the two for the sake of the one—but it's still a very delicate tightrope to walk. Because of family therapy, we have an awareness of bad habits and some tools to help us that we didn't at first."

To move through the process of a family session and provide a clear outline for parents wanting to encourage family therapy—and perhaps even to initiate some discussions at home—let's take a look at one treatment model in particular and how it is designed to help families develop the three major skills of goal setting, effective communication, and effective problem solving. It's called Encompass, and it was developed by Dr. Paula Riggs, a professor of psychiatry at the University of Colorado Denver.[1] Based on more than fifteen years of clinical research, Encompass is an evidence-based treatment that integrates care of substance disorders and co-occurring mental health problems.

GOAL SETTING

Research shows that having dreams and long-term aspirations helps protect youth from substance-related problems,[2] so helping them pursue and achieve these things can prevent them from using substances and experiencing relapse.

For diehards of Stephen Covey's best-selling book, 7 *Habits of Highly Effective People*, this hearkens to Rule No. 2: "Begin with the end in mind." In other words, know your goals, because if you don't know where you want to go, you're not likely to get there. Habit No. 3 is "Put first things first," which should encourage us to prioritize the steps leading to where we ultimately want to be. Family members should know what their ideal situation, or goal, is and how they want to change things to realize it.

But remember: this is family therapy, so other people in the room have goals and aspirations of their own. Knowing about them is part of helping everyone be in a good relationship—which, again, is the most important tool parents have to influence their child. Goal setting touches on many of the relationship principles we've covered in previous chapters, including being caring and responsive, spending time together, and establishing clear expectations.

So how do therapists using the Encompass treatment model help families with their goal setting?

First they try to help everyone think about the changes they would like to see in their relationships. Then they ask teens to complete a questionnaire about how happy they are in eight aspects of their relationship with their parents. Their answers move along a scale from 1 (completely unhappy) to 10 (completely happy). The eight aspects are

- time spent with parents,
- allowance,
- communication,

- affection,
- support of school or work,
- emotional support,
- general happiness, and
- general home activities.

Encompass practitioners ask parents to complete a similar questionnaire about their relationship with their teenager.

With the survey results in hand, the therapists ask everyone to present a family goal by answering the following questions:

- Which one thing would you like to change in the family?
- Why is this change important?
- What is the first step you can take toward this goal?
- What is the next step another person could take toward this goal?

It is very important for each family member to speak for himself or herself. It is recommended that they stick with "I" statements that employ communication skills outlined and encouraged in chapter 3. Many of these communication skills are derived from an excellent book, *Nonviolent Communication: A Language of Life* by Marshall Rosenberg, Ph.D. Using "I" statements means instead of saying, "You need to be more responsible and do your own dishes," try "I want the dishes to be cleaned before we all leave home for the day. This is important to me because I do not want our house to smell of dirty dishes and because I don't want dishwashing to be the first thing I think about when I get home. To make this easier, I will take care of my own dishes and leave the cleaning supplies near the sink. I would like it if you would rinse your dish and put it in the dishwasher after you finish eating."[3]

Next, therapists using the Encompass treatment model ask everyone to say three things they appreciate about each family member present. This step is an important reminder to families that they cannot let the positives of their relationships get lost in negativity that will sorely compromise their ability to reach goals. Making even just a few minutes to speak directly and sincerely to each family member about the specific things for which they're appreciated and loved does wonders to rebuild relationships.

Finally, Encompass therapists ask each person to write down his or her one family goal for the week—along with reasons for this goal, the steps that can be taken immediately to meet the goal, and the names of the people who can be counted on for help achieving it.

As the week progresses, family members also make time to write down the steps they took toward their goal and the positive steps they saw someone else in the family make toward the goals too. These observations are discussed in the following session.

PARENTS WHO HAVE BEEN THERE

"As a family, every single January 1, we all would sit down and write out our short-term, long-term, and mid-term goals," said Lisa Taylor, the mother in Colorado Springs who has grappled with a son's addiction. "It was a tradition the boys really liked. We would have our goals pasted under our mirrors, and my sons would cut out pictures from magazines to illustrate them.

"But once my oldest got to the end of middle school, that's when he didn't want to join us in this exercise anymore. He said it was stupid— and I could tell that he lost a lot of focus and sense of direction. I'm convinced that was about the time his drug use was getting way out of hand.

"Now that he's living on his own, we have a very different relationship—but he's coming back to me to talk about goals again. We've even written some of them down and put them on his refrigerator.

"That might sound like such a small thing, but I'm choosing to celebrate it."

EFFECTIVE COMMUNICATION

Yes, let's think in terms of C.R.A.P.—which, in this context, stands for "Communication resolves all problems."[4] Young people often laugh at the acronym—but whatever it takes to make them remember the concept, right?

When we communicate effectively, we're listening as much as getting across our points. In chapter 3, we also outlined smart approaches to communication as described in *Nonviolent Communication: A Lan-*

guage of Life by Marshall Rosenberg, Ph.D. For the sake of supporting family therapy sessions, these concepts are worth emphasizing:

1. Be calm. If you or the other person is upset, cool down first. People who are angry usually do not listen well or communicate effectively.
2. Express your feelings. This will make you humble and vulnerable—and it will be easier for others to relate to how you're feeling. Use true emotions with "I" statements such as "I feel upset" or "I feel exhausted" instead of "I feel like grounding you" or "I feel you don't listen to me."
3. Express your needs. The next step is to make clear the unmet need that leads to upset feelings. This step usually starts with "because . . . " For example, "I feel upset because I want you to excel at school." Or "I feel exhausted because I stayed up late waiting for you, and I need more sleep." Examples of statements that do not express needs are "I need you to respect me" or "I need you to be obedient." When you are tempted to say these things, think about the true need behind this. When you do so, the first statement might become "I want you to take the trash out every Tuesday." The second statement becomes "I want you to come home by midnight on weekends."
4. Convey understanding of feelings and needs. It's important to understand your child's feelings and needs. However, understanding is not enough. You have to convey that you understand. Here is how this type of listening might go:

Adolescent: You're always on my back and nagging me.

Parent: So you feel annoyed about things right now.

Adolescent: Yes, people are always on my case.

Parent: That must be pretty upsetting.

Adolescent: I want people to just leave me alone.

Parent: So you're pretty angry and you want me to ask you about your homework less often.

Adolescent: Yes.

It's important to note that the narrative above does not mean the parent necessarily agrees with the teenager and that he or she will indeed ask about homework less often. However, it does mean that the parent at least understands and communicates that understanding to the adolescent. This technique does wonders to foster calm and productive communication.

There are many communication pitfalls to avoid—and they include the blocks to listening identified as part of Attachment Communication Training (ACT) detailed in chapter 3. During family therapy sessions, these are common trouble areas that sidetrack discussion. They are consistent with ACT and with Dr. Rosenberg's method of nonviolent communication.

1. Giving advice: "Just do it this way" or "Cheer up. It's not so bad."
2. Educating: "This will teach you to do things differently."
3. Consoling: "How were you to know things would turn out like this? It's not your fault."
4. Storytelling: "When I was a kid, the same thing happened to me."
5. Interrogating: "What happened? When? Where? Who?"
6. Explaining: "I would stop asking you about your homework, but . . ."
7. Correcting: "That's not true. This is how it all happened."

These discussion traps do not lead adolescents to believe they are understood. As a result, a young person is more likely to find the process of communication frustrating, and he or she will simply stop talking. This, of course, harms the relationship and recovery process.

Expressing emotions well is a crucial element of communication because it helps a person convey honesty, sincerity, and humanity. However, discussing emotions can be difficult. Below are some common mistakes when expressing feelings and ways to consider correcting course:

1. "I feel you don't care." This statement makes an assumption about how the other person feels. Try "I'm sad" instead.

2. "I feel you don't understand me." This statement also makes an assumption about the other person. A better way to frame it: "I feel very alone."
3. "I feel like a terrible mother." This statement makes a value judgment. Preferred: "I feel guilty."
4. "I feel disrespected." Parents often make this statement—which makes an assumption about the listener. Use instead "I feel upset" or "I feel hurt." Just because someone begins a sentence with "I feel . . . " doesn't mean he or she is expressing an emotion. A true feeling does not involve a judgment or assumption about the other person, but a genuine, internal feeling instead.

Insight from the World of Recovery

"We had to learn how to communicate," said Joe G., the young adult in substance recovery in Saint Louis. "My parents had laid down their strict line: 'We love you, and if you use, you can't live here. We will not watch you do this to yourself.'

"I'm glad now that they communicated that much clearly, but we had a lot of other things to work out about our interaction. It was important for my parents to start letting go of some things without creating so much distance that they communicated they didn't care. That was hard for them, but they eventually were willing to loosen the reins and let me learn what I needed to once I was in the hands of people they felt they could trust.

"Sure, I was a ghost in my house for a while, but I wasn't dying," Joe said with a laugh. "For us, happiness was always in the gray areas. The more patient they were, the more I would tell them. Eventually I started staying home more again—and I was more open and honest with my parents than I ever had been and ever would have been had we not learned how to communicate with each other.

PROBLEM SOLVING

The main objective of the third family session is problem solving. In chapter 5, we discussed ways parents could help protect their children from substance use. Many of these protective factors can be influenced by healthy problem solving. Here are basic steps discussed as part of the Encompass treatment[5] model:

1. Recognize that a problem exists.
2. Identify the problem.
3. Brainstorm various ways to resolve the problem.
4. Select the most promising solution.

In session, families are asked to identify a problem they might like to work out. To get started, they consider the steps listed above. Sometimes it's helpful to start with smaller and easier problems and work up to more upsetting problems as the process gets easier. This family session also builds on the previous two sessions in that the problems are usually related to goals the family has identified and is working to address using the communication skills outlined above.

If things don't go well the first time, keep practicing. Stick to the plan. A lot can be learned from failed attempts. The key is to persevere.

THE TREATMENT PROVIDER'S PERSPECTIVE

"I say it all the time to parents: don't expect much of a relationship with your kid until they're sober," said Mike Weiland, the substance abuse counselor in Saint Louis. The treatment program he directs, called Crossroads, provides individual therapy to young people and twelve-step support groups for youth and parents. "Let your kid get sober and keep cleaning up your own stuff while he does. A lot of parents blame everything on their kid getting high—but once that kid is sober, they're still faced with the things they didn't address about themselves.

"When these kids are getting sober, a lot can also change about the family. These really beautiful people are coming out, and in time, they're genuine and really sweet. But it's not unusual to see parents and siblings have to work through their own resentment of having been subjected to so much pain and suffering."

"Oh, man, those resentments are deep," said Frank Szachta of the Crossroads Program, whipping out the digital copy of Alcoholics Anonymous's *Blue Book* that's always on his mobile phone. He landed on the sixth chapter:

"The alcoholic is like a tornado roaring his way through the lives of others," he read. "Hearts are broken. Sweet relationships are dead. Affections have been uprooted. Selfish and inconsiderate habits have kept the home in turmoil. We feel a man is unthinking when he says that sobriety is enough. He is like the farmer who came up out of his cyclone cellar to find his home ruined. To his wife, he remarked, 'Don't see anything the matter here, Ma. Ain't it grand the wind stopped blowin'?'

"Addicts create all of this turmoil and destruction and burden on the family, draining resources from parents and siblings. The resentments among everyone involved go with this territory.

"In early sobriety, young people are still equally self-absorbed, and sometimes worse. Life was unmanageable for them before they started getting drunk or high, and they just poured alcohol and drugs on everything as a solution to the problems that were making life so unmanageable. Take away the drugs and alcohol, and now you've got a young person who has no easy solution and no strong tools to use yet to deal. So there are times in the process of recovery when things are getting worse before they get better, and that time can be just as difficult for parents and siblings to deal with.

"During my first six months of sobriety, that was me," Szachta continued. "I was in meetings, meetings, and more meetings, totally self-absorbed, and my parents were neglecting my little sister, going to meetings of their own to save me. I remember her telling them she almost got high just to get their attention."

DISCUSSION QUESTIONS

- *Which one thing would you like to change in your family?*
- *What is the first step you can take toward this goal?*
- *What is the next step another person in your family can take toward this goal?*
- *What is the best way for you to ask your adolescent what he or she would like to change about your family?*
- *What is one thing you appreciate about your child?*

7

HOW PARENTS CAN HELP THEIR ADOLESCENTS NOT USE SUBSTANCES

The previous two chapters laid the foundation for what parents can do to help their adolescents and themselves make the most of treatment. Now let's consider in more specific detail how to put those concepts into practice at home.

As we've already established in chapter 2, the most important thing parents can do for their adolescent with a substance problem is to maintain a positive, warm, and loving relationship with him or her, because this is the most important tool parents have to shape their child's values and future directions. This doesn't mean parents seek to become a buddy or a new best friend. It means consistent communication—both in word and deed—that parents love their children whether they're using drugs or not using drugs, whether they succeed or fail, whether they are gay or straight, whether they are healthy or unhealthy, whether they're making good grades or failing every course. We're talking unconditional love here—but that also doesn't mean you have to be happy about, like, or agree with all of the choices your child makes. It just means you love your child no matter what.

As we also covered in chapter 2, parents should maintain communication, monitor friends and whereabouts, and create a drug-abuse-free home. Chapter 5 detailed the importance of establishing boundaries and limits that provide guidance by communicating values and expectations ("walls") and by clarifying absolutely nonnegotiable offenses ("shots").

These efforts to prevent drug use and addiction are also the steps that can be taken to prevent substance relapse—but now let's take a look at everyday decisions that actually make parents accomplices, or enablers, of their child's drug use, often unwittingly. Before getting into the nitty-gritty, common sense tells us two things: negative consequences may result from poor decisions and behavior. Logical consequences help us learn, and they include embarrassments, scoldings, punishments, failures, and hurts. When parents move to shield their children from reasonable negative consequences, they're not only giving them a pass to continue making the same mistakes, but they're also stymying their abilities to choose between right and wrong. Children must be allowed to make their own choices and to feel the gravity of them. That's just a part of growing up.

THE TREATMENT PROVIDER'S PERSPECTIVE

"There is a real aversion to the idea of suffering in our culture in general and a general misunderstanding that some of the suffering we go through makes us better people," said Father John Bonavitacola from his offices in Arizona. "We can learn something in those times and come through them stronger, kinder, more compassionate, more understanding, and smarter. That's a part of life. So don't shield your child from every single negative consequence and pain."

Love and permissiveness are not synonymous. Loving someone doesn't mean you have to accept their misbehavior or agree with their actions. A parent's love offers time, wisdom, personal conviction—and guidance through the establishment of limits and boundaries. Permissiveness accepts bad behavior. Parents are often afraid to impose limits because they fear making a problem worse. However, if they do nothing, chances are good the problem only will become more serious.

THE TREATMENT PROVIDER'S PERSPECTIVE

"Parents do their children a great disservice when they accept wrong behavior," said Frank Szachta, director of the Cornerstone Program in south suburban Denver. "It's important for parents to ask themselves what is motivating their permissiveness. Is it that they want to respect their child's space? Do they fear their kids will perceive them as a tyrant who pushes views and values down their throats? Maybe they think kids should be able to do their own thing and make their own way in the world.

"All of those lines of thinking are common, and they're approaches that definitely help kids grow up on their own, but they still don't actually explain a parent's permissiveness—or willingness to accept bad behavior. Permissiveness is instead motivated by three things in part or combination: parents want to be liked. Parents want to like themselves. And being a parent who stands up to wrong behavior and provides the guidance a child needs in a particular situation takes too much time and energy."

"You have to be a parent, and parenting is hard," said Amy Weiland, a substance abuse counselor at the Cornerstone Program in Missouri. "It means saying no. It means having your kid yell at you and call you a jerk. But that's okay, because they're testing boundaries and limits and deciding which side of them they want to be on. That's what they're supposed to do. They're teenagers."

Enabling is a difficult concept for many parents because practically all parents want to give their children good things. The problem is that sometimes parents give in a way that supports unhealthy behaviors. Parents in recovery often share the moments they first realized something about their actions enabled their child to continue using drugs. Among those pitfalls:

- They give their teen "lunch" money that gets used to buy drugs. Avoid giving teens more money than they need for a day or two—and know how their money is spent. Require receipts and pay directly into accounts benefiting your child.
- They give computers and cell phones, which are used to connect with drug-using friends and drug sellers. Mobile communication is a privilege, not a right. Adolescents should earn access to mobile technology through good behavior, which includes not using substances. As previously mentioned, parents should establish clear rules—and unapologetically monitor their child's digital communications at least occasionally. Review your billing statements to know whom your teen is texting and how often. Review

the applications he or she has downloaded on your dime—and know how they work not by asking your teen but by researching them on the Web.

- They give their teen a ride to a friend's house where the teen plans to use drugs. Diversion of drugs from friends is common—and diversion from the parents or siblings of your child's friends is not unusual. This is where vigilant parenting will require extra work. Never drop off your child at someone's home without taking even a few minutes to meet with the adults in charge, and make clear you do not want your child leaving the premises without your explicit permission.

- They leave town, and their teen throws a party in their house. It's a good idea to avoid leaving your adolescent—especially when he or she is early in sobriety—without a chaperone. Trust is earned and should not be granted too quickly.

- They allow their teen to spend too much time that is unaccounted for. Prosocial activities—such as sports teams, after-school clubs, social causes, and volunteer organizations—help your child build confidence and skills, make friends, and spend time focused on something other than drug use. At the same time, group outings can be covers for drug use, so be informed of logistical details and work with your child to establish appropriate times and ways for check-in.

- They take their teen out of treatment early because the teen complains about it. We're not talking about suspected cases of malpractice. We're talking about the kind of complaining that many adolescents use to wear down their parents until they get what they want.

- They allow teens to use or keep drugs in the house. If you want your teen to stop using drugs, then you do not allow your teen to use or keep drugs in your home or in your yard.

- They keep alcohol and other drugs in the house. "If my son has an allergic reaction to strawberries or peanuts, I'm going to clear my house of those foods, right down to pictures of them on the wall," said Mike Weiland, the substance treatment counselor in Saint Louis. "I am strong about this one. This is a show of solidarity with a child who needs a parent to protect them, not confront them every day with temptation."

- They pay for expensive lawyers to get their children out of trouble and/or bail them out of jail. There is a time and place for paying for lawyers and springing for bail, but parents need to ask if they are doing so in a way that enables continued substance use and criminal behavior, such as drug dealing, driving under the influence, stealing, or vandalism.
- They pay for a car used to go to parties, buy substances, and hang out with friends who use substances. Like mobile devices, vehicles are a privilege, not a right. Unlike mobile devices, vehicles can easily kill others and do every day. Parents should periodically monitor their child's vehicle and limit access until their adolescent has earned the trust required to use it.
- They engage in unhealthy emotional relationships with their children's peers. It is common for young people struggling with substance use disorder to be drawn to other young people with mental health and substance problems. Parents often unwittingly sabotage their own child's ability to resist drug use and other unhealthy relationships when they, too, play into them. "I've gotten beaten up for not being compassionate," said Jo McGuire, a Colorado Springs mother who has a son with substance addiction. "But I had to learn not to be a rescuer."
- They make excuses for their children when they know they're making excuses. Common examples are when parents contact their child's school to say an absence or tardy was excused when it really wasn't, and when they find themselves telling "white lies" about why their child couldn't make good on a commitment.
- They gauge too much according to school performance—or general performance. "As long as our daughter was making good grades, we thought we had no reason to ask about drug use," said Rino S., a Colorado father who is helping his daughter in early-stage recovery. "Boy, that was a big lesson. Good grades ultimately mean nothing if your child has a drug addiction. I can now see how people with drug problems tell themselves their drug use is okay as long as they're a good student or they're fine at work."
- They permit the consumption of drug-glorifying media. Yes, media are practically everywhere, but we're not powerless to reject them. We can say no to music, movies, software applications, publications, television, and any other programming that promotes

drug use. Parents can certainly prohibit these media from entering their home—and enforce consequences when their rules are broken. They also can refuse to pay for entry to events where drugs are consumed—and bar their children from going. Regular Internet research will help parents learn more about artists and media owners who advocate for drug use and its broad social acceptance.

INSIGHT FROM THE WORLD OF RECOVERY

"My interest in music and the shows I watched were all stereotypical of stoners," Raymond N. said. "The entertainment industry has a lot to do with what leads you to think drugs are fine, and what keeps you thinking they're fine and that anyone who tells you otherwise is nuts or out of touch with progressive thinking. There are so many big influencers of drug culture among kids that it's hard to pinpoint a few, but glorifying drugs or sneaking in references to how harmless and every day and okay they are has become commonplace—especially for pot. It's barely even mentioned as a problem, and even when it is referred to that way, it's all one big joke. It's something people just roll their eyes and laugh about. It's not taken seriously.

"Adults may not get all of the punch lines and references, but kids get every one of them," he added. "It was always so obvious to me what the deal was with companies marketing fast food at midnight or having people talk with sock puppets about the food they needed to order. When they made those commercials, they were marketing straight to people who smoke pot."

- They buy clothing and accessories that are popular in the drug culture. "It's amazing how quickly drug-using kids can find each other, but a lot of times it's what I call the 'drug uniform' that makes it so easy," said Jermaine Galloway, an officer with the Boise, Idaho, Police Department. He travels the country to teach community groups and parents about aspects of drug use and the drug culture under the motto "You can't stop what you don't know."[1] Officer Galloway encourages parents to be aware of the brands their children seek in clothing and accessories if for no other reason than to demonstrate that they're paying attention and interested in learning more about what their kids find cool and compelling. "When parents are putting clothes away, they may see brands they don't recognize," he said. "I recommend they just start looking up things on the Internet. They'll be able to tell if that brand is popular in the drug world."

- There are also items of clothing and accessories designed with "stash pockets" convenient for hiding drugs. Parents should search the term online for a look at how hats, jackets, pants, shoes—and pretty much anything else a teen might want to wear—are fashioned to conceal substances and help with the evasion of drug tests. "I can't emphasize enough how important it is to start a conversation with your child, not an interrogation," Officer Galloway said. "Context is everything, and parents just need to find out what a particular word or design means to their kid. They may find that the boy didn't know the significance and thought it was cool and wanted to be associated with the crowd. Every kid is different, and everything means something different to everybody. So no need to overreact or feel you have to be a police officer. All you have to do is pay attention, because not taking the small stuff seriously is what gets us into trouble. Drug problems start small. Someone didn't care or take use seriously, and then it got to a point of 'Oh, crap, how did we get here?'"
- They readily dismiss signs of drug abuse in their home. If there's one piece of advice for parents universally offered by those who have experienced and/or treated substance addiction, it's this: trust your gut. When stories sound improbable and things don't feel right or look right, or they seem a little off or out of place, it's time to ask questions and investigate. When items are missing around the house, or money is missing from wallets, investigate.

PARENTS WHO HAVE BEEN THERE

"You're not just looking for baggies filled with a leafy substance," said Jo McGuire. "A lot of times, things were staring me right in the face, but I didn't know what I was looking at.

"Kids will turn just about anything into tools they can use to smoke or huff. My son collected toilet paper rolls that he shoved into a drawer and told me he was using for a project. I believed him.

"Then dishes went missing out of the kitchen, and I would sometimes find glassware or scorched soda bottles in our backyard," she said. "Then he started asking for air fresheners, hand sanitizers, and wipes practically every time I went to the market. That one got past me for a while because my son has a mental health history consistent with obsessive cleaning—but he was trying to remove the odor.

"Then it was his excessive use of body sprays—although I noticed he wasn't looking cleaner.

"These things didn't happen all at the same time. They happened over time, so it wasn't immediately obvious to us. You feel so stupid when all the pieces fall into place, but no one wants to imagine their child is doing drugs. It's easy to come to every conclusion other than the one you should."

Among the items, uses, and places people in recovery say parents should stop to consider when they encounter them at home unexpectedly:

- lighters
- tinfoil (used to make a pipe)
- paper clips (to clean pipes)
- eyedrops, nasal sprays, breath fresheners, and body deodorants
- air fresheners (to cover up smells)
- dryer sheets (to cover up smells)
- eating utensils (to clean pipes)
- Missing electronics and other items of value. "I would go into places where we would store small electronics and other things we needed only occasionally—things like e-readers or DVDs—and they were always missing," said Lisa Taylor, whose son struggles with addiction. "He was taking them to pay for drugs."
- Screens missing from water faucets. "It's not as common for kids to use screens nowadays, but sometimes I hear about it," said Mike Weiland, who spent his own teenage years hiding marijuana from his parents in their home. "That's how we could always tell the pothead houses, because the screens, which are used at the bottom of a pipe as a filter, were missing from every sink."

- Speaking of screens, study those in the windows of your child's bedroom. "My mom caught on to problems when she figured out that was resin on my bedroom screens," Weiland said. "I would blow everything out the window—and always in the same place, I guess."
- "You can make bongs out of everything in the refrigerator," Weiland added. "When a container turns up in an odd place, ask about it."
- nails (to clean pipes)
- Stockpiles of pill bottles, which could mean your child isn't necessarily taking his prescription medicine but is selling it instead.
- Loose air-vent covers—which may be removed regularly to hide a stash.
- "Potheads keep seeds and stems, they collect weird things," Weiland said with a chuckle. "And you can massively smell marijuana on clothes, so if your kid has a sudden interest in doing his laundry and is totally insistent about that, investigate."

Nowadays parents also need to know about new marijuana products, such as vaporizers that come in the form of pens, highlighters, and asthma inhalers that make it easy to conceal the drug. "A mother who was paying attention to her son really impressed me," Officer Galloway said. "She discovered he had hollowed out a highlighter pen and was stuffing weed in there. I asked how she thought to even look. She said, 'One day, it finally occurred to me that he always had a highlighter on his calendar, and he always had one with him—but I never actually saw him use a highlighter for anything. Not once.'"

Parents should also look up on the Internet things such as marijuana wax, bubblegum, and dabbing. Dabbing is a very potent way of using marijuana that is becoming more popular and involves the use of potentially dangerous paraphernalia, such as a blowtorch. Finally, marijuana and butane hash oil can be put into almost any food product, including gummy bears, candy, brownies, and sodas as well as lotions, creams, and eyedrops. Parents will need to know about these products so that they can monitor their household more effectively.

Trust your instincts and say no to the wrong kind of enabling. At first your teen or young adult may complain more loudly about your new approaches and outlook. This is common and is called an extinction burst, which is a technical way of saying the teen is trying to call your bluff. Your relationship—and other household dynamics—are likely to get worse before they get better, but hold fast and stay strong. Do not enable your child to use drugs by giving them the money, time, or space they need to do so.

THE TREATMENT PROVIDER'S PERSPECTIVE

"Do enable your child to embrace sobriety," said Father John Bonavita-cola, pastor of Our Lady of Mount Carmel Parish in Tempe, Arizona. "Can you create a drug-free home where your child really wants to be, where he or she says, 'I love it here, and I don't want to do anything to screw it up.'? Can you offer that place where your children want to bring their friends over? That place where they feel loved and trusted and allowed to be a child in the home, which doesn't operate with two different sets of rules, one for adults and one for kids, because the adults know they must be role models and willing to set certain things aside? Can you provide the place where kids realize they don't need drugs to make them feel good or happy?

"Every day, we see families playing huge games of tug-of-war. Your teen will always win that game, so put down the rope, parents. Kids want to feel loved, that they can talk openly and don't have to hide from moms and dads who are too scrupulous or dogmatic, and that they have some freedom to do their own thing. When they get those things at home, that's a happy place for them and the best kind of prevention."

"People pay, but they don't pay attention," said Frank Szachta. "Sometimes you have to quiet the mind enough and devote your whole attention to your child even if they don't know that's what you're doing. Are you feeling how they feel? Are you really looking at them? Is there something you're uneasy about because it feels like something more than normal teen angst? Parent instincts are very accurate a lot of times. After all, you and your child really do have a powerful connection—believe it or not."

INSIGHT FROM THE WORLD OF RECOVERY

"Every single example you cite I have used, or it has happened to me, or I have watched it happen to an acquaintance," said Raymond N., a young man in substance recovery in Saint Louis. "What for me it all came down to was a lack of personal responsibility. The kids I was hanging out with didn't know personal responsibility and didn't care about right from wrong, and a lot of their parents weren't setting the greatest examples for them and the rest us, either. They kept substances in their home, and it was easy to get whatever we wanted. Or they were checked out and self-absorbed and ignoring all of the clues. Or they suspected problems, but they were scared to say anything or didn't know how to say anything or just figured it was all a phase and that their kid would work himself out as long as his grades are good. In all of those homes, they let the kid do whatever and come home and never face any consequences or major responsibilities at all. It's like everyone in their own way thought their kid would figure things out for themselves."

"Parents have to make sure their kids aren't putting on more shows for them," said Joe G., a young man in substance recovery who says his "smooth talking" helped him evade a lot of punishments he actually deserved. "The art of performance is what gets a lot of families into this trouble in the first place. They played roles. They weren't being real with each other. Everything—even their happiness—was artificial. So parents have to feel confident that their kids aren't driving responsibly, or not saying bad things on Facebook, or not filling their minds with songs about weed because they told them not to do those things or because their kids know they're watching them. Parents have to make sure their children understand *why* these things are unacceptable and *why* it's important that they don't do them. Then they need to stop being so controlling and let their kids make decisions and live with the consequences. As important as it is to be a vigilant parent, it's as important to have a well-informed, principled kid who understands why his behavior matters to himself, his family, and others. If your kids can't own those decisions for themselves, they won't own them when you're gone."

DISCUSSION QUESTIONS

- *How might you make it easier for your child to use drugs? How could you make it more difficult?*
- *If your teen complains about treatment, how do you plan to address him or her? What do you think you could or should say to encourage continuation?*
- *How might your child's behavior result in negative consequences, and how will you prepare to help him or her navigate them? How can you build a home your children want to come home to and invite their friends to be in?*

8

ADDICTION IS A CHRONIC CONDITION THAT REQUIRES CHRONIC MAINTENANCE

Because addiction is a chronic, relapsing disorder, families would be wise to establish a strategy for preventing relapse—and a plan for dealing with it when it happens.

Chances are that relapse *will* happen. After residential treatment, about 80 percent of adolescents relapse within the first six months of discharge.[1] These setbacks are upsetting and demoralizing to everyone involved—but they're also opportunities for families to restate their commitment to, and love for, each other. People struggling with addiction, regardless of age, need to hear love, patience, and empathy first—then accountability in the forms of consequences and boundaries on the swift follow-up.

People are not cured from addiction any more than people are cured from diabetes. When someone gets diabetes under control by taking insulin, we do not encourage him or her to discontinue that prescription. Instead we consider insulin an effective treatment and encourage its regular and responsible use. We should approach addiction similarly. When people get their lives under control through treatment, support groups, and other activities, we need to encourage them consistently to stick with the principles, people, and places that helped them turn their lives around. Too often youth go to treatment, get well for a short time—and then stop using their new skills and habits. They relapse soon afterward.

The temptation is for everyone to say a treatment didn't work when that's not true. As people in Alcoholics Anonymous often say, "The program works if you work it."

INSIGHT FROM THE WORLD OF RECOVERY

"If your kid is sober, and they have healthy peers who have been with them through much of their recovery, and then it appears they're finding reasons and ways to distance themselves from that good peer group, look out," said Joe G., a young adult in recovery in Saint Louis. "When I've seen relapse, it's always like that. Someone has lost connection with the people who helped them get sober.

"I will graduate from this program I'm in, and when I do, I'll be at AA meetings with sober people, because that is going to help me because those real connections are what I need to cope."

"I got sober almost two years ago, and I haven't relapsed," said Nell C., who is a young woman in recovery in Columbia, Missouri. "Why hasn't that happened? Honestly, I think it's by the grace of God, because there have been times when I have done everything else but drugs. I think I haven't gotten high because I have found a new definition of love. The drugs tell you that you know the 'real' love and the 'real' honesty and have the 'real knowledge,' but those are all lies. I know what it's like to be completely honest now. I know what it's like to have people who love me for who I am—and my happiness and friendship are all they want from me."

One of the reasons Amy Weiland is such a popular substance abuse counselor with young people living throughout Missouri is that she struggled with addiction as a teenager too. "There's a common saying in AA meetings: 'While I'm in here, my disease is out in the parking lots, doing pushups.' The disease is taking every opportunity to get stronger and to find ways to work on me," she said. "That means I have to work harder to build the protection it cannot penetrate, because while I may have another drink in me, I don't know if I have another 'getting sober' in me. People know what it takes to get sober, and that just makes it harder to do so again.

"The first time I relapsed, I was more concerned by how many people I had let down," Weiland continued. "And I was so bummed that they meant so much to me. I didn't want to have to tell my friends—especially not my new friends who had done so much to help me in recovery—that I had done that. So when I relapsed, I quickly realized that my biggest fear was having to tell my new friends in sobriety. That's when I started to realize that recovery was becoming important to me."

PARENTS WHO HAVE BEEN THERE

"Are we smarter guards against relapse now?" mused Starr S., a Colorado mom whose daughter is in recovery. "We have experienced it, so I can tell you that there has been no magic shield that has kept us safe from it, but the things we've learned along this road to recovery have been very helpful to our decision making. The best thing to come from these low points is the increased honesty about what was going bad before the use happened. I have also realized that I cannot take relapse personally, because it was not done to hurt me. In fact, it had nothing to do with me. We drop that idea right away and go forward.

"My husband and I always felt that our daughter's best chance was still with us, offering supervision and support and working to get the best help available. We've stayed that course, regardless of whether she does.

"As for offering advice about this to other parents, I would say, 'Explore your treatment options.' Insurance plans may want to see a thirty-day program, but we have been going to treatment for a year and a half now, and we have no intention of stopping anytime soon."

"This is why people in AA say they're twenty-seven years recovered," said Jo McGuire of Colorado Springs. "They know how hard it has been to maintain sobriety and how every day is a new battle. You don't conquer an addictive personality, and that's something I struggle to wrap my head around. At the core, addiction continues to replace itself, and it's just a question of what the next replacement is going to be. Maybe it's playing video games, gambling, or smoking, but then again, maybe it's eating well, running, and embracing positive attitudes.

"To other parents, I always say, 'Recognize that you're in this for the long haul, and even though everyone gets their support, you're never going to be able to let down your guard entirely. You're not going to ever be able to say that addiction problem is all better now, and we're so glad that's over. That is not what this looks like.'"

Good "recovery protection plans" involve families because, unfortunately, addiction affects everyone. Substance treatment isn't just about sending someone off to be repaired. It demands changes of a whole family system and the larger environments in which it operates. Fair or unfair, everyone has some work to do—which is why the continuation of family therapy and/or therapy for individual family members could be very helpful.

Here is one version of a recovery plan designed for parents. Though it provides a sound framework, consider this plan a starting point for discussion. Every family is different, and your plan isn't going to look like anyone else's. In order for this plan to work, it needs to be kept in a visible place, practiced daily, and updated at least monthly. Parents can make this plan on their own or consult a therapist. Ideally, parents get their teen's input by asking, "What can we do to help you stay clean?" What the teen says can provide valuable information for the final relapse prevention plan.

OUR RECOVERY PROTECTION PLANS

Now that your teen/young adult is clean, you need to think about what you will do to maintain these gains once you are done with treatment.

The first thing to do is to remember the reasons you started substance treatment. It is important to remind yourself periodically about how bad things had become and what is likely to happen if things go back to how they were. Write down those things in a notebook, journal, or some other spot where you can refer to them.

Consider how things have improved since your teen stopped using substances. Write those things down as well. You can continue to keep notes and journal entries to map your family's progress, your child's progress, as well as those things that can result in setbacks.

Maintaining these gains is hard work. You will have to work on maintaining these gains every day. As a general rule, if achieving results takes X amount of work, then maintaining those results takes double that amount of work. Here we want you to think of specific ways you will help your son or daughter stay clean and how you will help maintain the positive changes that are happening in your family. We encourage you to be specific. For example, don't write, "I will be a better listener." Instead write, "I will spend time every day trying to understand how my child is doing." List the things you will do and refer to them frequently. Check in to see how many things you follow through on, those things that work, and those things that don't.

Attendance at Al-Anon or Nar-Anon can be helpful for parents of teens in recovery. Think about the extent to which these programs will be a part of your family's recovery plan.

Are you planning to attend Al-Anon or Nar-Anon meetings?
Do you have a sponsor?
If yes, what is his/her first name and phone number?
Write down the time and address of the meetings you plan on attending.

Families with drug and alcohol problems tend to isolate themselves. They frequently don't talk to people about what they are experiencing—but as people in twelve-step programs often say, "We are only as sick as our secrets." Do not tell everyone about your family's problems without discretion. However, invite trusted people into your life who can understand and help. Opening up to them about problems will often relieve a lot of pressure.

Write down the names and phone numbers of friends and family you can talk with if you think your family's recovery is in danger. Make this list available to anyone who might need to refer to it.

Let people in your support system know how they can be helpful to you. Again, be specific. For example: "Please call me once a week for the next month to check in and see how I'm doing." Write down how people can be helpful and let them know. Most good friends and family members, professionals, and other supportive people will be happy to help.

Relapse is a process that typically begins before the actual substance use starts. Share the following signs of possible relapse with your support network. Ask the supporters you've listed to let you know if and when you and other family members appear to be slipping into old ways. If all of you know what to look for, you stand a much better chance of preventing relapses. Here are some warning signs. Make a copy of this list and refer to it often.

1. Telling people that you are "fine" or "okay" even if you are not
2. Blaming others for your problems
3. Becoming angry or resentful
4. Feeling anxious or stressed
5. Thinking things could never go back to the way they were
6. Deciding the only thing needed is for your teen not to use substances
7. Feeling depressed
8. Not having fun, leisure, or recreational activities
9. Being very busy
10. Living in the past or future, not the present
11. Overanalyzing things
12. Doubting there ever was a problem
13. Losing hope or believing your problems have no solution
14. Becoming overconfident
15. Making major life changes
16. Avoiding talking about signs of relapse
17. Talking about signs of relapse too much
18. Having trouble with forgiveness
19. Dwelling on past mistakes and hurts
20. Allowing or encouraging substance use "in moderation" or use of a substance that was not the original "drug of choice"
21. Thinking you, your child, or your family is cured
22. Panicking or giving up if there is a slip or lapse
23. Decreasing communication in the family
24. Avoiding problems
25. Being bitter or resentful
26. Losing your temper
27. Being passive or aggressive in your communication
28. Drifting away from an authoritative parenting style and being afraid to confront misbehavior
29. Not requiring your teen to do chores
30. Losing your expectations about substance use and other behavior
31. Spending less time with your teen
32. Not spending time validating and understanding your teen's thoughts, feelings, and needs

If you monitor yourself carefully and give your support system permission to be honest with you, you will know when you have stopped working on your recovery and perhaps have started to relapse. You should also ask your teen how you can help him or her maintain sobriety. Don't ask only once. Instead revisit the issue periodically.

Because relapse is always a possibility, consider how you'll respond when it happens. With whom will you speak, and where will you turn for help? Your plan might include talking with your son or daughter about getting back into treatment.

Ideally, you'll share this plan with members of your support network so they'll know how they can be specifically helpful. Write your plan of how to deal with a potential lapse or relapse.

Consider the various situations—such as social environments and family interaction—that might trigger old behaviors. For example, parents sometimes get very angry if their child misses a curfew. Other parents might rush to overprotect their children when they miss a class or have legal trouble. Write down possible situations that could bring back old ways of acting and how you hope to respond to them.

It has been said that failing to prepare is preparing to fail—and that's certainly true when it comes to helping anyone manage recovery. This plan isn't just something your teen must implement. It's something parents have to work on too. Treatment should lead to new ways of communicating, interacting, and living life—and it often will. The key to maintaining those positive changes is to plan sound and swift responses to anything that could compromise them.

THE TREATMENT PROVIDER'S PERSPECTIVE

"I spend a lot of time helping young addicts learn how to live with addiction and change it to make their lives healthier," said Josh Azevedo, a certified addictions counselor in Arizona who directs The Pathway Program. "We help a lot of young people ask themselves why they would want to go back to substances when their life is better. In recovery, they need plenty of time to slow down and focus on how they feel good when they've been a good older brother, or about how they really enjoy music and can play it so much better now, or about how that good grade they made is the result of their hard work and determination to make it.

"They have to learn the importance of reflecting on all of the things that bring them contentment and peace. We want them to stick there and add to that list for the rest of their lives, because if they already feel good about themselves naturally, they're not going to reach for a chemical substitute to feel that way."

"For young people, relapse is often part of the recovery process, and one of the chief reasons for that is because young people have not built up a lot of damage or unmanageability in life yet," said Father John Bonavitacola, whose Catholic parish in Arizona provides support programs for teens with addiction. "Teenagers just don't have the evidence that they have a problem as much as someone who has had a divorce or two and lost three jobs. It's much easier for them to rationalize their drug use and to play games with their addiction.

"They say things like, 'I had a problem with this substance, but not this one, so I'll try this one instead,' and so they go down.

"The strategy for parents should be to make that downfall as short as possible. Whatever consequences there are should come quickly and hard, because this is not the time to start softening consequences and systems of accountability. This is the time when it's best to raise their bottom as fast as you can—and that is what I have seen work best many, many times."

9

TAKING CARE OF YOU

In general, what is good for parents is good for teenagers. So it's important for parents to take care of themselves and each other.

As we've established, parents can do many things to influence their teen's substance use—and several are linked directly to parental self-care:

- Having a supportive marriage can improve one's parenting.[1,2] As established in chapter 5, if a spouse feels supported and understood, he or she has more patience and strength to handle tough situations. Think about how to keep your marriage or relationship as positive as possible and take the steps to do so. To do this, it is important to have quality time when you agree to focus on each other, not the substance abuse problem.

- Teens learn a lot about life by imitating the adults around them. You are a role model, and you teach your child how to live healthily by living healthily yourself.[3] Teens learn many things through observing their parents. Examples include how to have a healthy marriage, healthy eating, balancing hard work and leisure time, managing money, fitness, sleeping, calm communication and problem solving, assertiveness, living with integrity, and much, much more. Therefore, it is important to lead by example in many areas of your life.

- The more you take care of yourself, the fewer resentments you will have. With fewer resentments, you will be more patient, calmer, and better equipped to handle the tough job of parenting. Too frequently, parents sacrifice all their time, energy, and money for their children. They do this because they love their children. However, when parents give at the expense of their own emotional health, they run the risk of emptying their emotional gas tank. They often become angry and resentful and give up on their child who is having problems. Frequently, this happens just as a family is finally sitting down to start treatment. It's not unusual for parents to express that they're giving up before they've even had the chance for treatment to help them. To avoid this situation, it's important for parents to pace themselves and to continue doing things they enjoy. Remember that helping your child is a marathon, not a sprint. So seek out your own social supports and interests so you can have interests and an identity that don't revolve around the substance use disorder.

THE TREATMENT PROVIDER'S PERSPECTIVE

"Dealing with someone who has addiction can become so draining and bleak, but we have to help people move from that place where they think their future is so bright they need a flashlight," said Frank Szachta, director of the Cornerstone Program in metro Denver. "I call them 'the look-forward-tos,' and whether it's something big or small, I want everyone looking forward to something. I ask what they're looking forward to that weekend or the next month. I want them making plans. Life has to go on."

It is also common sense that the healthier and more supported you are, the more you will be able to listen to your child, validate and understand his or her feelings, take on the difficult task of confronting bad behavior, spend time with your family, and control your temper. It's common sense that if someone listens and supports us, we have more to give someone else.

So remember what the airlines tell us during all of those preflight safety checks: "Adults, put your oxygen mask on first, and then assist your child." You're not making a choice between taking care of yourself or helping your children. Taking care of yourself *is* helping your children.

Focus on what you can do to make things better. Parents of substance-abusing children often beat themselves up. "I should have known my son was using drugs so much earlier," they often say, or "I shouldn't have let this happen." Good therapists will remind these parents early and often to think differently. After all—and as mentioned throughout this book—parents can do everything right and still have a teen who has a substance problem. While feeling guilty is normal, it is not helpful. Guilt leads to many emotions and behaviors that hurt recovery, including anger, bitterness, resentment, overprotection, enabling, loss of hope, passiveness, decreased caring, lack of clear-headedness, fear, and impatience. A little anxiety about how addiction hurts teens and their families can be motivating. However, guilt tends to paralyze. So when you feel guilt coming on, try to focus on what you can do in the here and now to help yourself and your family.

PARENTS WHO HAVE BEEN THERE

"We didn't realize how much of a grip my son's addiction had on us until he was gone," said Jo McGuire, the Colorado Springs mother whose son moved to another state, where he continues to struggle with substance use disorder and co-occurring mental health problems. He rarely visits. "If family plans and your entire family structure are beginning to revolve around your one child's responses, reactions, and preferences to prevent any and every negative outcome, it's time to step back and assess how you can regain control of that situation.

"My husband and I had to inject some normalcy into our lives—and into the lives of our other children," she continued. "We went to plays and dinners and on all sorts of other outings to have days when we weren't focused on addiction or even on him.

"At one point, he had moved out, and after some time away with sporadic communication, he wanted to move back in," McGuire added. "He decided to ask us about this in the days leading up to a family vacation we had planned. We had to tell him that the timing of his request was in conflict with that trip and that we would be happy to talk when we returned. We gave him access to our house—but we also confirmed that he was not invited to join us on our trip.

"He was furious. 'How could you do this to me? You want me to get clean, and you say you're going to be there for me, but you're leaving me stuck and alone!' He laid the guilt on thick—and we were feeling guilty in no time flat. But in that moment, my husband and I also realized what we were doing to ourselves—and to our other children—again. If our son had gone with us, it would not have been a vacation for any of us. He would have been there, controlling everything. We held our ground, and it was very hard. But you have to be determined."

Here are examples of how parents can take care of themselves. Self-care should be positive and healthy in the near and long terms. Sure, shopping, or "retail therapy," may feel good, but it can be tough on the household budget and cause different problems. Taking care of oneself looks different for different people, so some of these examples may or may not be a good fit for you:

- Ask directly for assistance with household chores. Contributing to the household in some way helps teens feel like productive, important members of the family. Sometimes it can be difficult to get teens to contribute. If this is the case, start small, be creative, and persist. There must be something your teen can contribute to the household.
- Insist that older teens work and pay rent or contribute to family expenses.
- Take care of physical needs, such as getting good sleep, eating healthily, and exercising.
- Have regular, adult conversation with someone who can listen and support you emotionally. Ideally, this is your partner. However, it may also include a professional therapist or a support group.
- Have regular date nights with your spouse or partner.
- Take care of your spiritual needs through prayer, meditation, mindfulness, fellowship, giving thanks, and worship. There is a reason why Alcoholics Anonymous and Al-Anon include a healthy dose of spirituality that encourages rebirth and new beginnings. A common saying in these organizations is "Let go, and let God." This slogan may have different meanings to different people, but in general, it implies a letting go of things that are not directly under your control. Such release can be liberating. Of note, AA and Al-Anon are spiritual but not religious. This distinction is very

important, because it allows for the inclusion of people of different faiths, even atheists who believe in a greater good or collective
consciousness.

- Let go of things you used to do for your teen, such as waking him
or her up in the morning, washing clothes, and providing transportation. It's time to let your child assume more responsibilities
and to have to live with the consequences of making poor decisions. Perhaps some of the things you do for your teen not only
consume your time and energy but also enable your teen to keep
using substances. Check yourself regularly to make sure you are
not enabling continued drug use and revisit chapter 7 for a refresher on some of the ways parents commonly enable their children. When in doubt, ask your partner, therapist, or members of a
support group for an objective opinion about whether or not you
are an "enabler." A general rule of thumb is, don't do for your
children anything that they can do for themselves.
- Get a massage, haircut, or manicure.
- Pursue a hobby. This sets a good example for your adolescent.
- Enjoy simple pleasures, such as reading, watching a television
show, enjoying a cup of coffee, or wearing your favorite tie or
dress.
- Meet with other parents who are going through, or have been
through, similar situations. By doing this, you are likely to get
emotional support, good ideas, and a realization that you are not
alone.
- Find things to be grateful for. When you are grateful, you're more
positive.
- Give back what you've learned, because it reminds you where
you've come from. This involves helping other people who are
going through what you experienced. Doing this will not only help
others but will remind you how far you've come and how bad
things could be if you are ever tempted to stop the lifelong recovery process.

A good way for parents to monitor the effectiveness of self-care is by
tracking their mood and energy. Feelings of tiredness and resentment
are a good sign that more self-care is needed.

INSIGHT FROM THE WORLD OF RECOVERY

"I didn't decide to give up drugs myself," said Joe G., a nineteen-year-old in Saint Louis. "The breaking point for me came when it came for my mom—when she did what she decided she had to do to take care of herself.

"After my parents divorced, my mom had my brothers and me, and she was overwhelmed. I have an autistic brother at home, so I think she dismissed what was going on with me as a phase and told herself everything would be fine as long as I was doing well in school.

"But then she was testing me, and I was failing drug tests all the time and getting into fights. There were empty bottles and bottles of pills in my room in all of these hiding spots. And then she'd catch me in lies just about every day.

"One day, my mom finally told me I couldn't live with her anymore because she couldn't take care of me, watch what I was doing to myself—and also pay for it all. I got really out of hand, and she locked me in my room. I told her I would hurt her and my brothers if she didn't let me out. She called the police, and I took a trip to a psych ward.

"I'm a smooth talker, so I was there for only eight hours. I talked with officers and doctors, and by the end of the night I was able to just leave. I didn't have to be admitted—but under the conditions my mom set, I had the choices of intensive inpatient treatment or outpatient treatment. I chose the one-on-one counseling option.

"My mom found a counselor who met with me first and somehow managed to bring her guard way down immediately. He even got some of my freedoms restored! That forced me into a situation where I felt I had no other choice but to listen to what he had to say. I never got high again."

A WORD ABOUT CARING FOR SIBLINGS OF DRUG-ADDICTED YOUTH

For many of the same reasons and in many of the same ways, the sober brothers and sisters of drug-addicted adolescents also need to be encouraged to take care of themselves. Their parents can help them a great deal with this by giving them the love, time, and attention they deserve. This is important, because youth tend to go to where the attention is. It doesn't matter if the attention is positive or negative. Attention is attention, and youth crave it. So make sure you reward good behavior in other siblings who are not using substances by giving them a healthy dose of attention. It's also possible that your teen who is using substances will see the positive attention that the other siblings receive and want to receive some of that for themselves. Giving attention to siblings who are doing the right thing will also lead to less resentment on their part for the tornado that addiction causes within families.

Siblings are obviously important to family therapy sessions. They may also wish to pursue their own time to speak with a therapist or to attend a support group where they can connect with other young people sharing similar experiences.

THE TREATMENT PROVIDER'S PERSPECTIVE

"When you've got a kid who is essentially killing themselves, it's easy to leave your other kids on a back burner," said the Crossroads Program's Amy Weiland, who, decades later, remains saddened that her own teen substance problems took so much of her parents' attention away from her siblings. "You have to give all of your children an avenue to talk about what's going on at home—and you, the parent, may not be the one they want to talk to.

"I meet with the siblings of my clients on a regular basis, and I usually start off with a summary that is meant to disarm them, make them laugh, and validate their feelings of frustration and resentment:

"'So, I bet your mom and dad are giving him sooooo much attention, but he's just a total asshole, and now his treatment is probably going to make it harder for them to pay for college for you, too, and even worse is that now that he's sober, he's still an asshole, but one who walks on water as far as your parents are concerned.'

"We have to cut to this chase as quickly as possible, because what no one wants to see is a sibling making his or her problems bigger just to be heard. Maybe that kid doesn't get high, but because the parents are so distracted, he could be doing everything short of using drugs to get attention."

It is imperative for parents to recognize that they may have to deal with incredibly difficult circumstances to take care of themselves and their other children. Parents may even have to fire some, if not all, of the six shots representing their nonnegotiables—as explained by the Cornerstone Program's Frank Szachta in chapter 5. Asking a child to leave home is the last shot.

THE TREATMENT PROVIDER'S PERSPECTIVE

"I have known many parents who have asked their children to leave home," Frank Szachta said. "I will never tell a parent to make this demand. I will discuss options, and I will move to empower the parent once they have determined they have reached this point. Usually I see very sad people who have done everything they can and have given the young person every opportunity they think is appropriate. These parents feel they have no other reasonable alternative, so either working as a couple or as a single parent, they have determined this is the most loving thing they can do at this moment for their child and to protect themselves from endless abuse.

"Maybe this is the point of despair that gets through to a teenager and encourages change, or maybe this is one more step they need to make to reach their bottom," Szachta said. "Whatever it is, the sooner they reach that point of despair, the better."

A SIBLING'S PERSPECTIVE

"That was a terrible day," said Sarah, a young adult from Colorado who was still in high school the afternoon her older brother called her upstairs to admire the guns he had recently stolen and stored under his bed. She knew her brother's drug and mental health history. He had started using marijuana when he was in the seventh grade, and at one point he had expressed a desire to kill their family.

"I knew I had to call my mom and dad at work right away, but I waited for my brother to leave our house. I was so scared. In just a matter of minutes, they were both in his room, looking at the guns. My brother had filed the serial numbers off them.

"Mom and Dad knew they had to call the police. They had to do it for my brother. They had to do it for the rest of us. My dad even works in insurance, and he could have lost his professional license if he hadn't handled all of this honestly with the authorities.

"The police officers came, and when they understood the situation, they were so nice. They were obviously trying to help us, even my brother.

"My brother came home while the police were still there, and he started yelling that he hated me and that he couldn't believe I had said anything. He said anything bad that happened to him was going to be all my fault.

"My parents asked him to leave our house that day. They had been dealing with him for years. They had tried everything. So we made food, and we packed a lot of his clothes and shoes. My dad assured him that he would stand by him in the legal system and that we would go through all of that together. He just couldn't live at home anymore because he had chosen to do something that had to result in these consequences.

"Later, I thought about how I had been my brother's caretaker for many years and when I was way too young. All those times he would get drunk or high and need someone to put him to bed or cover up for him at school. I was always taking care of that stuff, and I couldn't manage it anymore. For the longest time I felt guilty about my role in what happened that day. But in time, I realized it had to happen, and I'm glad my parents protected us."

PARENTS WHO HAVE BEEN THERE

"Why did we call the authorities? We felt it was important for our daughter to experience the gravity of the consequences of her actions," said Starr S., the Colorado mother who, along with her husband, works diligently to secure addiction treatment for their daughter. "Had we shielded her and given her that pass, she would have been right back at it, I am sure. Getting the law involved woke her up and got her attention in a way I don't think anything else could have.

"She was bored in high school—an A student—and she realized she could get away with a lot. She had a persona no one would suspect, so she thought of herself as the perfect person to get away with it all.

"The day we found everything in her bedroom—syringes, pill bottles, just everything—and realized she was selling was devastating," she continued. "I got advice as quickly as I could from people I really respected, including professionals in education like me. A lot of them told me to just throw it all away and say nothing. Get her the help she needed, but get rid of everything, and don't call the police.

"They were persuasive, but I just couldn't do that. I had to go with my gut. I kept thinking about all of those kids' names on the pill bottles we found. I knew some of them and could see they were somehow involved—so this was not just our family's problem, and it was bigger than we could handle on our own.

"I have been with her as she has had to navigate the legal system—and that was always the deal: 'I am turning you in, and I am standing with you the rest of the way.'"

DISCUSSION QUESTIONS

- *How are you going to take care of you this week? What about your spouse or partner? What about your children who do not have addiction?*
- *Have you experienced feelings of guilt about your child's substance use? What triggers those feelings, and how can you avoid those triggers?*

10

ADVOCATING FOR ADOLESCENT SUBSTANCE PREVENTION

Once parents feel their lives are manageable again—whether that's with a child in the throes of addiction or one who is in active substance recovery—they often find it helpful for their continued recovery to help others. Offering this support can be a great reminder of how bad things were and how far the family has come.

Connecting with people who are not as far down the never-ending path of recovery also can help you and your family guard against slipping into old habits.

For these reasons and many more, Al-Anon's twelfth step involves carrying the message of recovery to others: "Having had a spiritual awakening as the result of these [eleven other] steps, we tried to carry this message to others, and to practice these principles in all our affairs."

But how to do so is different for different people and varies with experience, passion, talents, and time. Let's take a look at a few ideas for getting started and finding a good fit.

Al-Anon and other twelve-step programs provide built-in systems for attending meetings and sponsoring other people. But if you're not involved in such a program, your twelfth step could involve extended family, your neighborhood, faith communities, and local schools. The opportunities to serve others are practically limitless. Here are just some of the efforts made by parents in recovery and advocates for those in substance recovery nationwide:

- They've started social media groups on networks such as Facebook and actively share the information published by other groups championing sobriety and recovery.
- They've organized drug prevention presentations for other parents at their child's school.
- They've trained the family dog to earn a therapy dog certification, so they can take their pet into clinical settings to soothe people in treatment.
- They've used their professional expertise to serve on the boards of nonprofit organizations devoted to helping people in recovery—or they've at least found enough time to help around their offices with filing.
- They've organized fund-raisers for treatment and recovery support causes—or they make it a priority to attend the annual events hosted by organizations that could use financial support.
- They've alerted neighbors and fellow voters about proposed legislation that could affect drug use at the local, state, and federal levels.
- They've written notes of thanks and encouragement to the people who have helped them in recovery.
- They've supported their nearest community drug-prevention coalitions—and if they don't have one nearby, they form one.
- They've volunteered to chaperone "sober-social events" for young people and have offered after-school tutoring for them.
- They've engaged in news coverage and opinion making about drugs and drug policy. They have written letters to newspaper editors. They have called reporters, asking for more frequent or more accurate and fair news coverage about how drug use harms individuals and communities. They have pressed for corrections and clarifications of news reports. They have left comments online, sometimes challenging the accuracy and fairness of a story or column. They have offered to write guest opinions on the editorial pages of local publications.

INSIGHT FROM THE WORLD OF RECOVERY

"At this point, what keeps me sober is helping other struggling addicts and alcoholics," said Joe G. "When I first showed up at support groups, I needed a whole lot of help—and I still do because if I go back to making things all about me, then something is going to fall. I would like to do a lot of work in psychology, and I wish there was more emphasis on addiction treatment in medicine today. I think medicine has emphasized too much on pills and lacked great focus on real, human solutions to drug use and addiction. So I'm excited to get started with my studies—and to tell my story and use it however it might help people. Give away what you were given to help others."

PARENTS WHO HAVE BEEN THERE

"My personal experience in walking through adolescent addiction recovery, and parent recovery, has shaped my life in ways I never could have imagined," said Theresa Henry, of Saint Louis. Her son is in substance recovery. "None of us will ever be the same again—both in positive and limiting ways. Today my heart is centered on this population, and as a parent steering-committee member for an adolescent substance treatment program, I spend a great deal of intimate time in recovery with dozens of youth and their families every week.

"As I watch these young people come out of the fog, I see how they struggle with so many of the things they typically say 'other kids just get'" because they were sober—not high, suspended, or expelled from school; dropped out of school entirely; or spending time in the prison system because of drug-related crime.

"They're embarrassed and ashamed by their lack of practical life skills in just about every arena, including personal hygiene, interpersonal communication, time management, organization and planning, résumé and job application writing, budgeting—and, well, you name it. They're also understandably eager to do life on their own and often have a hard time taking their parents' advice, no matter how well-meaning it is.

"Sadly, these young people are emotionally vulnerable and at great risk for relapse when their self-worth continues to suffer for lack of practical life skills. Across our country, there is a stark absence of community support to help young, newly sober people—and that's where I'm now focused. I am using my own professional background in occupational therapy—the work of helping people participate in the things they need and want to do in life—to bring enhanced recovery options to young people and help them achieve independent success as quickly as possible."

"Education is definitely the key to prevention, and I have decided to talk to anyone who will listen about how drug use affects families," said Lisa Taylor, the Colorado Springs mother who son continues to grapple with substance addiction. "I am teaching a class in my community every other week for the next several months about marijuana and its impact on families and communities. I'm also working on a master's degree, and my thesis involves the impact of marijuana legalization on Colorado. The more people I meet, the more I learn about how marijuana has affected so many children and families who counted on schools, local government, the federal government, and the media to inform them about how dangerous this addictive drug can be. They feel let down, and so do I—but we're committed to getting the truth out there. More of us who have struggled are coming forward."

ADVOCATING FOR RESPONSIBLE PUBLIC POLICIES

The United States needs more parents who have lived with the nightmare of child addiction to demand big changes in public policy. Understand that what is happening outside your house affects what happens inside it too—and that those with financial and political interests wrapped up in the sale of addictive recreational drugs don't have much of a track record for caring about addiction's impact on your home.

Making matters worse is that access to quality mental health care is a major problem in this country. Research shows that only about 10 to 30 percent of youth with a substance use disorder actually access treatment.[1] This treatment gap is due in large part to the third-party-payer insurance system.

Traditionally, third-party payers have not covered addiction treatment and, when they do, reimbursement is minimal. The short-sightedness of this is staggering—especially given research that shows when treatment is paid for, teens go voluntarily and benefit.[2,3,4]

Even worse is that a lot of youth can't access the health care they need or get it paid for until they've done something so bad they're sent to a juvenile court, which will cover treatment costs.[5] That's nothing to make America proud.

Also troublesome is the United States' lack of treatment options that integrate care for psychiatric and substance use disorders. About 80 percent of youth in substance treatment have a co-occurring psychiatric disorder.[6] However, only 25 percent of youth in substance treatment receive truly integrated care.[7] This is despite expert guidelines that have called for integrated mental health and substance treatment since at least 1999.[8,9] This lack of integrated treatment also stems from a third-party-payer system that traditionally hasn't covered it, a lack of research in this area, and a shortage of providers who are trained in both mental health and substance treatment.

The need is enormous for advocacy around making quality treatments affordable and accessible to families and youth. The United States has profoundly inadequate treatment infrastructure to deal with the medical problems that come with expanded drug legalization and lax enforcement of drug policies.

COMMERCIALIZATION OF DRUGS, DRUG USE, AND DRUG CULTURE

Another issue that is mission-critical for drug policy advocates to understand is the harm commercialization of alcohol, marijuana, and tobacco has on individuals, communities—and entire nations. The commercialization of substances has led to marketing that directly targets and harms young people. Consider:

Eighty percent of alcohol and tobacco company profits come from heavy adult users.[10] And as discussed in chapter 1, almost all heavy adult substance users start using as adolescents. To give another example, 88 percent of adult smokers started smoking before the age of eighteen.[11] With respect to marijuana, one in six adolescents who try the drug before age eighteen develops a marijuana use disorder compared to one in eleven for those who start after the age of eighteen.[12]

And of the 2.4 million people in the United States who try that drug for the first time each year, 58 percent are under the age of eighteen.[13]

So there is big financial incentive to market addictive substances to youth. This helps explain why tobacco companies used cartoons in their advertising campaigns, ran contests appealing to teenagers, and splashed ads appealing to high school cheerleaders and young American soldiers everywhere. It is why marijuana companies today sell gummy bears, candy bars, coloring books, THC-infused knockoffs of popular kids' cereals, games, and vaporizers designed to look like highlighter pens at the same time they claim not to target young people.[14]

By appealing to youth, these companies generate young users, who turn into heavy adult users, who turn into profits. In the meantime, as we discussed in chapter 1, young people suffer disproportionately because of the impact substances have on their developing adolescent brains.

Arguing about whether sellers of addictive products *intend* to target young people is almost beside the point. Communities should push back on any practices and products appealing to kids, regardless of the sellers' intentions.

Currently, tobacco companies are making a comeback by selling electronic cigarettes, or e-cigarettes, that come in flavors such as cherry, cookies and cream, strawberry, and vanilla. These products are not harmless.[15] Compared to regular cigarettes, an electronic cigarette may contain up to 40 times the amount of nicotine, the primary addictive product in cigarettes.[16] Electronic cigarettes also may contain some of the same carcinogens and toxins as traditional cigarettes—such as acetaldehyde, acrolein, formaldehyde, and nitrosamines—and many additives that are undisclosed because they are not currently regulated by the U.S. Food and Drug Administration, or FDA.[17] There is reason to believe secondhand exposure to electronic cigarette vapor exposes nonusers to nicotine, volatile organic compounds, and other constituents of electronic cigarette vapor.[18]

Unfortunately, the prevalence of e-cigarette use nearly doubled from 2011 to 2012.[19] For the reasons outlined above, we should advocate for the FDA to regulate e-cigarettes. The agency regulates traditional cigarettes and has banned flavored cigarettes, which have been found to appeal to youth.

Another way youth are frequently introduced to tobacco is through hookah bars, where young people smoke sweetly flavored tobacco products, which are addictive and harmful to health and have been shown to appeal disproportionately to young smokers.[20] We should also advocate for tighter regulations and zoning for such establishments.

Then there's the current rush to commercialize marijuana—as if our country has learned nothing from its experience with Big Tobacco. Indeed, today's pot barons are taking just about every page from the playbook crafted by the barons of tobacco:

• They target youth. This is evidenced by products such as gummy bears, candy bars, and sodas as well as advertising that includes cartoon characters and video game fonts. Marijuana smoking is becoming popular in movies and television shows the way that smoking was promoted in movies. Cigarette smoking in movies has been clearly shown to influence onset of smoking in adolescents.[21]

• They overstate the drug's medical benefits and understate, if not entirely ignore, its harms. In 1930, American Tobacco ran an ad stating, "20,679 Physicians say that Lucky is less irritating."[22] These types of ads continued for several decades. Currently, marijuana is marketed as medicine for addiction, attention deficit hyperactivity disorder, cancer, depression, post-traumatic stress disorder, and much more despite evidence that marijuana can actually make some of these conditions worse.[23] Despite clear and consistent evidence, which was reviewed in chapter 1, the harms of marijuana are frequently downplayed. Many people even insist that marijuana is not addictive, that it doesn't impair driving, and that the drug is healthy and natural. A quick Internet search confirms these attitudes. However, science does not support these claims.[24]

• They spend a lot of money to buy policy. Finally, just as Big Tobacco spends a lot of money on lobbying, so does Big Marijuana. Research shows that in 2002, Big Tobacco donated $6.8 million to members of the U.S. Congress and that the amount of money received directly correlated with the representatives' voting record on tobacco.[25] Similarly, the Big Marijuana lobby is growing at the local, state, and federal levels.[26]

• They spend a lot of money to influence and buy media. Within one week of the *New York Times'* editorial board's call for the legalization of marijuana, the news organization published its first full-page ad promoting the drug from a company offering users' reviews of marijuana strains and sales outlets.[27]

This process is more fully summarized in an article titled "Big Marijuana—Lessons Learned from Big Tobacco," published in the *New England Journal of Medicine*, one of the world's most prestigious medical journals.[28]

Research in Colorado shows that legal marijuana is sold to minors either directly or indirectly on a widespread scale and that this highly potent marijuana is producing more severe addiction than before.[29, 30, 31] Despite the misleading "science" pushed out by the marijuana industry, we also have worrisome indicators that adolescent marijuana use may already be rising and that more people are driving and crashing under the influence of marijuana.[32, 33]

So what's the answer? It is helpful to look back in time. In the 1970s, drug use, including marijuana use, was at an all-time high. For example, the past-month prevalence of marijuana use among twelfth-graders peaked at 37.1 percent in 1978,[34] but by 1992[35] that number dropped to a low of 11.9 percent. How did this drop occur? Many people attribute the change to the "Parent Movement," which was reportedly born after a raucous house party in 1976. The couple who owned the home returned to find their teenage daughter had opened it to teens who left bottles of alcohol and drug paraphenalia behind. The couple contacted the parents of several teens who had attended the party—and while some were offended and hung up quickly, others were concerned and helped form a group of concerned parents. Together they created a movement to educate, raise awareness about, and push back at the commercialization and glamorization of drug use. Their work was successful—and is documented in two books published with help from the National Institute on Drug Abuse:

• Manatt, 1979, *Parents, Peers and Pot I*
• Manatt, 1983, *Parents, Peers and Pot II*

To summarize the steps the parent group made:

1. They trusted their instincts about the effects of substance use more than the messages sent by people who profit from the commercialization and marketing of substances.
2. They gathered as parents to discuss their concerns and form common goals.
3. They mobilized medical professionals to help educate principals, school nurses, teachers, and legislators about teen substance use.
4. They met with school leaders with the following attitude: "What can we parents do to improve the social experience of our teenagers?" Subsequently, they helped develop school curricula around substance use and diversion programs so teens caught with alcohol or drugs could receive treatment.
5. They agreed to talk with their teens about substance use and to enforce family rules to prevent substance use.
6. They became active. For example, they asked their elected representatives to create and enforce zoning laws that restricted the sale of drug paraphernalia; they wrote to inform companies about the way their trademarks were being violated by drug paraphernalia companies; they wrote letters to editors; they called the police to report drug-related violations; and they took out newspaper advertisements to express their concerns and ask people to join them.

By doing these things, parents prevented teen drug and alcohol use, saved countless lives, and changed the course of country.

THE TREATMENT PROVIDER'S PERSPECTIVE

"You know how I advocate besides prayer and care?" said Father John Bonavitacola, the Catholic priest ministering in Arizona. "I suggest people engage in the political process. More of us have to raise the flags until people get our point of view. I recognize that it is really hard in our individualistic culture to make the argument that there is a greater good and a community good that we all might have to sacrifice for—but I won't be silenced about that truth."

DISCUSSION QUESTIONS

- *What could you do this week or this month to advocate for people in substance recovery?*
- *How do you think the commercialization of drugs, drug use, and drug culture might affect your family?*

11

ADDITIONAL RESOURCES

This book aims to provide for parents a broad overview of issues related to adolescent substance use. Some of you may want more details and in-depth information. We hope this list of additional resources is helpful.

In chapter 1, we discussed the importance of teen substance use and the impact that substances can have on the developing adolescent brain. This is a rapidly developing field of study. To stay on top of it and other research, we recommend consulting the websites for the National Institute on Drug Abuse www.drugabuse.gov) and the National Institute on Alcohol Abuse and Alcoholism (www.niaaa.nih.gov). NIDA's website provides valuable information for teens, parents, educators, and scientists. The agency's website also includes a way to contact NIDA with questions that are not answered online. You may also want to follow NIDA on social media, including Facebook and Twitter, to receive regular updates.

We also discussed the developing adolescent brain and how substance use can affect this development. A helpful and clear review of the adolescent brain and the way it is changing is available in the book *Brainstorm: The Power and Purpose of the Teenage Brain* by Daniel Siegel, M.D. Understanding the adolescent brain and how it differs from the adult or child brain can help parents and other adults interact more effectively with teenagers.

In chapter 2, we discussed how to know if there is a problem and what to look for in treatment. One website that may be helpful is the

National Registry of Evidence-Based Programs and Practices (www. nrepp.samhsa.gov). This website lists treatments that have been shown to work in research studies. In most cases, contact information is provided for the researchers who developed these treatments. The researchers, in turn, should be able to tell you if their treatment is available in your area. There are good treatments that are not yet on this list. To help you navigate this path, NIDA also has a publication called *Seeking Drug Abuse Treatment: Know What to Ask*, which is available on their website.

Dr. Thurstone's preference for adolescent/young adult substance treatment is the Encompass program, which is an outpatient program described in the following website: www.ucdenver.edu/encompass. Encompass genuinely treats both substance use disorder and mental health problems in an integrated fashion. It is also an individual treatment, not a group treatment. Therefore, treatment is tailored to the needs of each teen and family. The individual treatment also protects against teens joining together to share information about drugs and drug dealers. The research-proven, active ingredients of this treatment include:

- cognitive behavioral therapy, which helps youth change the way they think, feel, and act;
- motivational interviewing, which is an empathetic, nonconfrontational approach that helps youth become motivated for positive change;
- integrated mental health and substance treatment, which addresses the whole person;
- case management to help youth become involved in positive activities that promote recovery;
- contingency management, which provides rewards and incentives to youth for providing clean urine drug screens, showing up, and getting involved in positive recovery activities;
- family treatment to assist with the principles discussed in chapters 5 through 9;
- medication-assisted treatment if needed to reduce cravings and withdrawal or treat co-occurring psychiatric disorders.

Contact the developers of Encompass through their website, and they can direct you to the nearest Encompass program and/or tell you how you could help advocate for this model of treatment in your city.

We have met and deeply respect many people involved in the Enthusiastic Sobriety Approach (www.enthusiasticsobriety.com)—and we have used many of their voices throughout this book to complement the findings of rigorous, peer-reviewed science. While "Enthusiastic Sobriety treatment" has not been studied scientifically, it relies on the common sense of the twelve-step approach that has helped so many people. One important caveat is that this approach to substance treatment does not generally support medication-assisted therapy—so if your teenager has a history of serious mental illness, or if you feel medications should be an important part of his or her recovery, then Enthusiastic Sobriety may not be the best fit. Our special thanks to Mike and Amy Weiland of the Crossroads Program in Saint Louis. Their program can be found online at www.thecrossroadsprogram.com. Frank Szachta's program, Cornerstone, can be found at www.thecornerstoneprogram.com. Father John Bonavitacola can be found at Our Lady of Mount Carmel Roman Catholic Church and School in Tempe, Arizona, http://olmctempe.com. The Pathway Program in Gilbert, Arizona, directed by Josh Azevedo, is online at www.thepathwayprogram.com.

In chapters 5 through 9, we discussed how families can help their teens not use substances. The general principles of family therapy that are helpful for teen substance abuse are called structural family therapy, developed initially by Salvador Minuchin. Unfortunately, we have not found a self-help version of this treatment, but having the name of its original developer may assist your research. Related to the communication skills we covered, we recommend learning more about Dr. Rosenberg's work and his book, *Nonviolent Communication: A Language of Life*. This book has helpful information about how to communicate effectively as a family.

Some of the principles we've discussed are also expanded upon in the book *Parent to Parent*, which is available through Meek Publishing (www.meekpublishing.com). This book contains a daily entry from parents who have been through the recovery process with their teenager struggling with addiction. This book has been very helpful both clinically and personally. Many of the principles discussed are consistent with

Al-Anon, a twelve-step organization that provides "strength and hope for friends and families of problem drinkers." Al-Anon has meetings, which provide much support and wisdom. We recommend attending these meetings, which can be located on their website: www.al-anon. alateen.org .

We also mention the importance of helping young people achieve "natural, earned highs" rather than chemically induced ones. We're big fans of Matt Bellace, a Ph.D. psychologist and comedian who has traveled the United States and Canada for nearly two decades to encourage more than one hundred thousand students every year to pursue natural highs and make healthy choices. You can find him online at www.mattbellace.com. His talks with students are positive, science based, and highly entertaining—and you can also learn more about them in his book, *A Better High.* "Young people need to feel empowered in their schools and communities," Bellace said. "It's not enough to ask them to stay away from drugs and alcohol. We need to show them positive things they can do instead, both for themselves and others." We couldn't agree more.

The Natural High Education Network is a fantastic resource for substance prevention educators, regardless of whether they're working in school classrooms or in community settings. The network's website, www.naturalhigh.org, provides motivational and inspiring videos featuring prominent people in a variety of fields who explain how they've found natural highs far more powerful than alcohol and other drugs. The network has also produced a curriculum that can be used in a variety of settings and is free for the download.

In chapter 10, we discussed the importance of advocating for adolescent substance prevention. This advocacy takes place at many levels: community, national, and international. At the local level, many communities have drug-free community coalitions, which are funded by the Office of National Drug Control Policy (ONDCP). These coalitions are listed on the ONDCP website (www.ondcp.gov). You could contact your local coalition as well as your state Office of Drug Control Policy (if your state has one) to ask how to be involved. Additionally, the National Guard has CounterDrug Task Forces throughout the country. These task forces have the mission to "reduce the supply and demand of illegal drugs through partnerships with law enforcement, community organizations and schools districts." Your local CounterDrug Task

Force can help connect you with local advocates (www. ngbcounterdrug.ng.mil). If your community does not already have a coalition, you can develop your own. The Community Anti-Drug Coalitions of America (CADCA) can provide you with the tools to start a coalition (www.cadca.org). The National Institute on Drug Abuse also has a publication called *Preventing Drug Abuse among Children and Adolescents* (http://www.drugabuse.gov/publications/term/95/Evidence-Based%20Practices). As mentioned above, NIDA also has two publications, *Parents, Peers and Pot I* and *Parents, Peers and Pot II*, which describe the successes of the Parent Movement. Parents may find helpful ideas and inspiration in these publications as well.

We also appreciate the Partnership for Drug-Free Kids, which provides an array of free resources aimed at helping parents determine whether their child has used drugs—and what to do about it if the suspicion is confirmed. You'll find the organization online at http://www.drugfree.org.

The National Association of Drug Court Professionals is found online at www.nadcp.org. The nonprofit organization seeks to reform problematic laws related to substance use and addiction and also advocates for drug courts that use a combination of judicial monitoring and substance treatment to compel drug-using offenders to change their lives.

Internationally, there are organizations whose work to prevent drug abuse and addiction worldwide we track regularly. Both the World Federation Against Drugs, www.wfad.se, and IOGT International, www. iogt.org, are headquartered in Stockholm, Sweden. Drug Policy Futures, which is found online at www.drugpolicyfutures.org, is led by a global steering committee of drug policy experts.

Dr. Thurstone has joined some of the United States' top addiction treatment specialists to serve as a science advisor for Smart Approaches to Marijuana, or SAM (www.learnaboutsam.org), a nonprofit organization cofounded by former U.S. representative Patrick Kennedy and world-recognized drug policy expert Kevin Sabet. SAM is an alliance of organizations and individuals dedicated to establishing health-first approaches to marijuana policy that decrease the drug's use and do not harm users with arrest records that stigmatize them for life, making it even more difficult for them to break free from cycles of substance dependence. On the issue of marijuana legalization, we also recommend Kevin Sabet's book, *Reefer Sanity: Seven Great Myths of Marijuana* (Beaufort Books). Finally, we keep an updated website for people who want the latest information on teens and addiction. The website is www.drthurstone.com.

12

SUMMARY

After a decade of treating adolescents with substance abuse problems and analyzing data sets related to this field, I am still struck by how much misinformation there is about adolescent drug use. Too many parents have been through the wringer of adolescent substance abuse and have arrived at specialty treatment through the most circuitous routes possible. The situation appears to be worsening now that a new industry, the marijuana industry, is promoting its products and services, too often targeting youth. For these reasons and more, my wife and I were compelled to write a book that guides parents with science and stories from people who have worked in this field even longer than I have.

This closing summary is designed to be a quick-hit reference parents can reach for over and over as new situations arise.

First, we discussed the importance of taking adolescent substance use seriously. Adolescents undergo an important period of brain development. Substance use—whether it's alcohol, marijuana, tobacco, or opiates, such as prescription pain pills—may permanently affect the way an adolescent's brain develops. Because of their developing brains, adolescents are much more vulnerable to becoming addicted to substances than are adults. In the vast majority of cases, addiction starts in adolescence. For every day, month, and year an adolescent doesn't use substances, he or she buys time for healthy brain development and a reduced chance of addiction. Unfortunately, the fact that young people are especially vulnerable to addiction is widely known by the alcohol, marijuana, and tobacco industries. This is why those industries have long histories of targeting teenagers with advertising and marketing—both directly and subtly. This is also why parents and other concerned adults in every community must know the science and do what we can to reject the forces that compromise healthy brain development for our youth.

We then discussed how to know if a young person has a substance abuse problem and what to do about it. First, it's important to remain calm. Anger and guilt usually make the problem worse, not better. If you believe your teen has used only once or twice and doesn't have any other problems, such as depression, then you can probably tighten your supervision and proceed without professional help. However, if you know your teen has used alcohol or other drugs more than a few times and/or has emotional problems and/or is not functioning well in school or social life, then you should get help immediately. Do not wait, and try not to ignore or dismiss what is troubling you. Substance use disorder is like cancer: the earlier it is detected, the easier it is to treat.

We also discussed the importance of having a healthy dose of skepticism. If your child says that he or she was only holding the paraphernalia for a friend, it's time to ask pointed questions. Early-onset substance users are usually very careful not to get caught. It's not until the substance use has progressed that teens get careless with concealing their use.

Next, we discussed the importance of effective communication as described by Dr. Rosenberg's book, *Nonviolent Communication: A Language of Life*. The basic strategy here is to remain calm and wait until your teen is calm before engaging in discussion. Then follow these steps:

First, communicate a genuine emotion, such as "I am upset."

Second, communicate your reason. An example: "Because I want you to grow healthy and strong."

Third, communicate your wish: "Please tell me how I can help you not use substances." Then listen and validate your teen's feelings. Too often, parents think validating their young person's feeling means they agree with them. This is not the case. Validation in this context simply means you communicate to your teen that you understand him or her. An example would be: "I can understand why you would want to use drugs because everyone else is doing them too."

If substance use is more than one or two occasions and/or there are significant emotional or behavioral problems, parents should seek treatment for their teen. Adolescents with substance abuse problems need specific substance treatment. There's no reason to believe treating co-occurring problems such as anxiety, depression, or self-esteem will make the substance abuse problem magically disappear. There are many nuances to treating adolescents with substance abuse problems that a specialist in adolescent addiction is qualified and equipped to address. For a referral to a specialist, parents can consult their primary care physician, school counselor, friends, or the Substance Abuse and Mental Health Services National Registry of Evidence-Based Practices and Programs. In general, parents should look for a program that uses an empathic approach, is evidence based, integrates mental health and substance treatment, encourages involvement with positive peers and activities, provides family treatment, provides ongoing continuing care to prevent relapse, and respects the adolescent's confidentiality. Treatment should last a minimum of ninety days and should be in the least restrictive setting that is safe for the situation.

In the middle of the book, we discussed the general principles of family therapy. The first step is to foster a positive, warm, and loving relationship with the adolescent. Ultimately, it is this relationship that influences the adolescent to assume the positive values of his or her parents. When in doubt, strive to have a positive, warm relationship that communicates, "I love you no matter what, no strings attached." After this, it is important to strive for an authoritative parenting style as opposed to authoritarian, passive, or neglectful parenting styles. Authoritative parents are warm and loving at the same time they set and enforce clear expectations for behavior. We discussed the different ways parents shape their teen's behavior through various types of rewards and punishments. Authoritative parents use a combination of different rewards and punishments without simply relying on punishment. They give their children age-appropriate freedoms and a sense of the consequences that could stem from their decision making. Other important concepts include helping teens find life, purpose, and meaning; setting a healthy example; communicating clear expectations; maintaining a healthy marriage or relationship (if applicable); involving teens in household chores; and involving extended family who can be helpful.

The three basic skills that are frequently covered in family treatment include goal setting, communication, and problem solving. First, it is very important to set family goals. By doing so, families can prioritize their actions to maximize their chance of getting to the place they want to be. It is again important to remember the skills of nonviolent communication as described in *Nonviolent Communication: A Language of Life* by Dr. Rosenberg. It's also important to remember the acronym C.R.A.P, which stands for Communication Resolves All Problems. Stay calm. Start with a genuine emotion and express a genuine need. Then parents need to listen and validate their teen's thoughts and feelings. Repeat—because this isn't always going to go well, but families often get better with practice.

Finally, we discussed the importance of effective problem solving. Instead of reacting in the moment, families are encouraged to step back, consider all options, and choose the most assertive approach.

It's crucial to remember that addiction is a chronic condition. It is not something that is cured and goes away. As it is commonly said in AA, "While I'm in here, my disease is out in the parking lot, doing pushups." So it is important to ask your teen early and often, "How can I be helpful?" Listen carefully and use the information to develop your relapse prevention plan for how you will help your teen stay clean and how you will help if there is a relapse. Don't fall into the traps of going back to social or "responsible" use of substances or substituting other substances that were not the original substance of abuse.

Sometimes parents wonder what to do about tobacco use. This is an important question, because about two-thirds of adolescents in substance treatment have co-occurring tobacco use, and smoking remains the leading cause of death in the United States. Research on adults in substance treatment shows that adults who quit smoking have better substance treatment outcomes.[1] Preliminary research shows that teens who reduce smoking during treatment also reduce use of other substances.[2] Therefore, tobacco use should generally be discouraged and certainly not enabled (in other words, avoid buying cigarettes for your teen). However, parents may have to pick and choose their battles, and in many cases tobacco use is not the most immediate concern.

At the end of the book, we reminded parents to put on their own oxygen mask first before assisting their young person. This means parents need to continue to take care of their own emotional health. They cannot focus on the substance use disorder all the time. They need to have a break every now and then to recharge their batteries. Not only will doing this help parents run the marathon, but it also will set a good example for their teenager.

Finally, I encourage parents whose home life has stabilized to help other families experiencing similar problems. Not only does this commitment help others, but it reminds families of how things used to be and motivates them not to slip into old habits. There are many ways to be involved. Current needs include being involved in a support group, advocating for access to quality treatment, and advocating for public policies that protect youth from becoming easy targets for the alcohol, tobacco, and marijuana industries. The options are endless for families wanting to use their unique gifts and passions to serve others.

BIBLIOGRAPHY

1969 draft report "Why One Smokes" to the Philip Morris board of directors. Document Bates No. 1003287836.

1970 (August 13) message from a Lorillard advertising account executive to a marketing
professor, soliciting help from his students with advertising design. Bates No.
92352889.

A 1973 RJR draft paper, "Some Thoughts About New Brands of Cigarettes For the Youth Market." Bates No 502987357-7368.

1980 report, "Apparent Difficulties and Relevant Facts." Bates No. 689753864.

Alati R., P. Baker, K. S. Betts, J. P. Connor, K. Little, A. Sanson, and C. A. Olsson, 2014, *Drug and Alcohol Dependence* 134:178–184.

American Academy of Child and Adolescent Psychiatry, 2005, *Journal of the American Academy of Child and Adolescent Psychiatry* 44:609–621.

ASCD, 2012, Making the Case for Educating the Whole Child http://www.wholechildeducation.org/assets/content/mx-resources/Whole-Child-MakingTheCase.pdf.

Bandura A., 1978, *Journal of Communication* 28:12–29.

Baumrind D., 1993, *Child Development* 64:1299–1317.

Beal, S. J., L. D. Dorn, S. Pabst, and J. Schulenberg, 2014, *Prevention Science* 15:506–515.

Beardslee W. R., and D. Podorefsky, 1988, *American Journal of Psychiatry* 145:63–69.

Bennett L. A., S. J. Wolin, and D. Reiss, 1988, *British Journal of Addiction* 83:821–829.

Brown S. A., A. Gleghorn, M. A. Schuckit, M. G. Myers, and M. A. Mott, 1996, *Journal of Studies on Alcohol* 57:314-324.

Business Insider, 2014, http://www.businessinsider.com/new-york-times-leafly-marijuana-ad-2014-8, last accessed August 2, 2014, 9:01 p.m.

Cabrera N. J., C. S. Tamis-LeMonda, R. H. Bradley, S. Hofferth, and M. E Lamb, 2000, *Child Development* 71:127–136.

Casey B. J., S. Getz, and A. Galvan, 2008, *Developmental Review* 28:62-77.

Centers for Disease Control and Prevention, 2013, *Tobacco Product Use Among Middle and High School Students—United States 2011-2012*.

Charlesworth A., and S. A. Glantz, 2005, *Pediatrics*, 116:1516-1528.

Chen K., and D. B. Kandel, 1995, *American Journal of Public Health* 85:41-47.

CNBC, 2014, last accessed February 3, 2014, http://www.cnbc.com/id/101886620.

Coleman L. G., W. Liu, I. Oguz, M. Styner, and F. T. Crews, 2014, *Pharmacology, Biochemistry and Behavior* 116:142-151.

Counotte D. S., A. B. Smit, T. Pattij, and S. Spijker, 2011, *Developmental Cognitive Neuroscience* 1:430-443.

Counotte D. S., A. B. Smit, S. Spijker et al., 2012 *Frontiers in Pharmacology* 3:1-6.

Crowley T. J., and P. D. Riggs, 1995, *NIDA Research Monograph* 156:49-111.

Degenhardt L., L. Dierker, W. T. Chiu, M. E. Medina-Mora, Y. Neumark, N. Sampson, J. Alonso, M. Angermeyer, J. C. Anthony, R. Bruffaerts, G. de Girolamo, R. de Graaf, O. Guereje, A. N. Karam, S. Kostyuchenko, S. Lee, J. P. Lépine, D. Levinson, Y. Nakamura, J. Posa-da-Villa, D. Stein, J. E. Wells,AND R. C. Kessler, 2010, *Drug and Alcohol Dependence* 108:84-97.

Degenhardt L., C. Coffey, H. Romaniuk, W. Swift, J. B. Carlin, W. D. Hall, and G. C. Patton, 2013, *Addiction* 108:124-133.

M. Dennis, S. H. Godley, G. Diamond, F. M. Tims, T. Babor, J. Donaldson, H. Liddle, J. C Titus, Y. Kaminer, C. Webb, N. Hamilton, and R. Funk, 2004, *Journal of Substance Abuse Treatment* 27:197-213.

Dickson P. E., M. M. Miller, T. D. Rogers, C. D. Blaha, and G. Mittelman, 2014, *Addiction Biology*, 19:37-48.

Elvis Duran on the Z100 Morning Show on Friday, November 8, 2013.

Everett S. A., R. Lowry, L. R. Cohen, and A. M. Dellinger, 1999, *Accident; Analysis and Prevention* 31:667-673.

Fergusson D. M., J. M. Boden, and L. J. Horwood, 2006, *Addiction* 101:556-569.

Fernández-Ruiz J., M. Gómez, M. Hernández, R. de Miguel, and J. A. Ramos, 2004, *Neurotoxicity Research* 6:389-401.

Food and Drug Administration, last accessed February 3, 2015, http://www.accessdata.fda.gov/scripts/cdrh/cfdocs/cfIVD/Search.cfm.

Gardner M. N., and A. M. Brandt, 2006, *American Journal of Public Health* 96:222-232.

Gass J. T., W. B. Glen Jr., J. T. McGonigal, H. Trantham-Davidson, M. F. Lopez, P. K. Randall, R. Yaxley, S. B. Floresco, and L. J. Chandler, 2014, *Neuropsychopharmacology* 39:2570-2583.

Gordon A. J., J. W. Conley, and J. M. Gordon, 2013, *Current Psychiatry Report* 15:419.

Grant B. F., and D. A. Dawson, 1997, *Journal of Substance Abuse* 9:103-110.

Grant, B. F., and D. A. Dawson, 1998. *Journal of Substance Abuse* 10:163–73.

Gray K. M., Carpenter M. J., N. L. Baker, S. M. DeSantis, E. Kryway, K. J. Hartwell, A. L. McRae-Clark, and K. T. Brady, 2012, *American Journal of Psychiatry* 169:805–12.

Gray K. M., P. D. Riggs, S. J. Min, S. K. Mikulich-Gilbertson, D. Bandyopadhyay, and T. Winhusen, 2011, *Drug and Alcohol Dependence* 117:242-247.

Hall W, and L. Degenhardt , 2009, *Lancet* 374:1383-1391.

Hall W. D., and M. Lynskey, 2005, *Drug and Alcohol Review* 24:39-48.

Hendershot C. S., R. E. Magnan, and A. D. Bryan, 2010, *Psychology of Addictive Behavior*, 24:404-414.

Hoeve M., J. S. Dubas, V. I. Eichelsheim, P. H. van der Laan, W. Smeenk, and J. R. Gerris, 2009, *Journal of Abnormal Child Psychology* 37:749–775.

Klein C., 2010, University of Rhode Island Inventory for Change Assessment and Substance Treatment Outcomes, oral presentation at the annual meeting of the American Academy of Child and Adolescent Psychiatry.

Jacobus J., L. M. Squeglia, S. Bava, and S. F. Tapert, 2013, *Psychiatry Research* 214:374-381.

Jager G., and N. F. Ramsey, 2013, *Current Drug Abuse Review* 1:114-123.

Johnston, L. D., P. M. O'Malley, J. G. Bachman, J. E. Schulenberg, and R. A. Miech, 2014, last accessed February 3, 2015, http://www.monitoringthefuture.org//pubs/monographs/mtf-vol1_2013.pdf.

Johnston et al., 2014, Monitoring the Future national survey results on drug use 1975-2013 Volume I secondary school students.

Kandel, D. B. P. C. Griesler, G. Lee, M. Davies, and C. Schaffsan, 2001, *Parental influences on adolescent marijuana use and the Baby Boom Generation: Findings from the 1979-1996 National Household Surveys on Drug Abuse*, Substance Abuse and Mental Health Services Administration.

Kumpfer K. L., and B. Bluth, 2004, *Substance Use and Misuse* 39:671–698.

Liddle H., and C. Rowe, 2010, *Adolescent Substance Abuse Research and Clinical Advances*.

Luke D. A., and M. Krauss, 2004, *American Journal of Preventive Medicine* 27:363-372.

Meek Publishing, 2011, *Parent to Parent*.

Meier, M. H., A. Caspi, A. Ambler, H. Harrington, R. Houts, R. S. Keefe, K.MacDonald, A. Ward, R. Poulton, and T. E. Moffitt, 2012, *Proceedings of the National Academy of Sciences* 109:E2657-2664.

Moffitt, T. E., M. H. Meier, A. Caspi, and R. Poulton, 2013, *Proceedings of the National Academy of Sciences USA* 12:E980-982.

Mokdad, A. H., J. S. Marks, D. F. Stroup, and J. L. Gerberding, 2004, *Journal of the American Medical Association* 291:1238-1245.

Monitoring the Future, 2014, last accessed February 3, 2014, http://ns.umich.edu/new/releases/22362-college-students-use-of-marijuana-on-the-rise-some-drugs-declining.

Monitoring the Future, 2014, last accessed February 3, 2015, http://www.monitoringthefuture.org//pubs/monographs/mtf-overview2013.pdf.

National Institute on Drug Abuse, 2012, *Principles of Drug Abuse Treatment*.

National Institute on Drug Abuse, 2013, Seeking Drug Abuse Treatment: Know What to Ask, last accessed March 11, 2015, http://www.drugabuse.gov/publications/seeking-drug-abuse-treatment-know-what-to-ask/introduction.

National Survey on Drug Use and Health, last accessed March 11, 2014, http://www.samhsa.gov/data/population-data-nsduh.

Newsweek, 2012. Last accessed March 11, 2014, The New Pot Barons: Businessmen bank on marijuana. http://www.thedailybeast.com/newsweek/2012/10/21/will-pot-barons-cash-in-on-legalization.html.

NHTSA (2008), last accessed March 11, 2014, http://www-nrd.nhtsa.dot.gov/Pubs/811169.PDF.

O'Brien, C. P., et al., 2004, *Biological Psychiatry* 56:703-712.

Officer Galloway, last accessed February 3, 2015, www.tallcopsaysstop.com.

Prochaska, J. J., K. Delucchi, and S. M. Hall, 2004, *Journal of Consulting and Clinical Psychology* 72:1144-1156.

Rabinoff, M., 2006, Ending the Tobacco Holocaust, Elite Books, Santa Rosa, CA.

Rhee, S. H., J. K. Hewitt, S. E. Young, R. P. Corley, T. J. Crowley, and M. C. Stallings, 2003, *Archives of General Psychiatry* 60:1256-1264.

Richter, K. P., and S. Levy, 2014, *New England Journal of Medicine*, 371:399-401.

Riggs P. D., and R. D. Davies, 2004, *Journal of the American Academy of Child and Adolescent Psychiatry* 41:1253–55.

Riggs, P. D., S. K. Mikulich-Gilbertson, R. D. Davies, M. Lohman, C. Klein, and S. K. Stover, 2007, *Archives of Pediatric and Adolescent Medicine* 161:1026-1034.

Riggs, P. D., et al., 2011, *Journal of the American Academy of Child and Adolescent Psychiatry* 50:903-914.

Riggs, P. D., S. K. Hall, S. K. Mikulich-Gilbertson, M. Lohman, and A. Kayser, 2004, *Journal of the American Academy of Child and Adolescent Psychiatry* 43:420–429.

Rosenberg, M. A., 2003, *Nonviolent Communication: A Language of Life.*

Rubino T., N. Realini, D. Braida, S. Guidi, V. Capurro, D. Viganò, C. Guidali, M. Pinter, M. Sala, R. Bartesaghi, and D. Parolaro, 2009, *Hippocampus* 19:763-772.

Salomonsen-Sautel S., J. T. Sakai, C. Thurstone, R. Corley, and C. Hopfer, 2012, *Journal of the American Academy Child Adolescent Psychiatry* 51:694-702.

Salomonsen-Sautel S., S. J. Min, J. T. Sakai, C. Thurstone, and C. Hopfer, 2014, *Drug and Alcohol Dependence* 140:137-144.

Schuermeyer J., S. Salomonsen-Sautel, R. K. Price, S. Balan, C. Thurstone, S. J. Min, and J. T. Sakai, 2014, *Drug and Alcohol Dependence* 140:145-155.

Science Daily, 2014, last accessed Febraury 3, 2014, http://www.sciencedaily.com/releases/2014/06/140627133057.htm.

Siegel, D. 2014, *Brainstorm: The Power and Purpose of the Teenage Brain*, Penguin Group, New York.

Silins E., L. J. Horwood, G. C. Patton, D. M. Fergusson, C. A. Olsson, D. M. Hutchinson, E. Spry, J. W. Toumbourou, L. Degenhardt, W. Swift, C. Coffey, R. J. Tait, P. Letcher, J. Copelan, and R. P. Mattick, Cannabis Cohorts Research Consortium, 2014, *The Lancet Psychiatry*, 4:286-293.

Simons-Morton B., 2004, *Addictive Behavior* 29:299–309.

Skinner, B. F., *Science and Human Behavior*, 1965.

Solinas M., L. V. Panlilio, and S.R. Goldberg, 2004, *Neuropsychopharmacology* 29:1301-1311.

Squeglia L.M., D. A. Rinker, H. Bartsch, N. Castro, Y. Chung, A. M. Dale, T. L. Jernigan, and S. F. Tapert, 2014, *Developmental Cognition and Neuroscience* 9:117-125.

Tobacco Free Kids, last accessed February 3, 2015, http://www.tobaccofreekids.org/content/what_we_do/industry_watch/product_manipulation/2014_06_19_DesignedforAddiction_web.pdf.

Tomlinson K. L., S. A. Brown, and A. Abrantes, 2004, *Psychology of Addictive Behaviors*, 18:160–169.

Thurstone C., S. Salomonsen-Sautel, S. K. Mikulich-Gilbertson, C. A. Hartman, J. T. Sakai, A. S. Hoffenberg, M. B. McQueen, S. J. Min, T. J. Crowley, R. P. Corley, J. K. Jewitt, and C. J. Hopfer, 2013, *American Journal on Addiction* 22:558-565.

Thurstone C., P. D. Riggs, S. Salmonsen-Sautel, and S. K. Mikulich-Gilbertson, 2010, *Journal of the American Academy of Child and Adolescent Psychiatry* 49:573-582.

Thurstone C., P. D. Riggs, S. Salmonsen-Sautel, and S. K. Mikulich-Gilbertson, *Drug and Alcohol Dependence* 118:489-492.

Thurstone C., M. Tomcho, S. Salmonsen-Sautel, and T. Profita, 2013, *Journal of the American Academy Child Adolescent Psychiatry* 52:653-654.

Tobacco Use Epidemic in the U.S.: Is 50 Years of Progress Enough?" Last accessed February 3, 2015, http://www.surgeongeneral.gov/initiatives/tobacco/

Treatment Episode Data Set, 2009, last accessed march 11, 2015, http://wwwdasis.samhsa.gov/teds07/TEDSHigh2k7.pdf.

Volkow N., 2014, last accessed March 11, 2015, http://www.youtube.com/watch?v=RSDnLSU3owc.

Wagner F. A., and J. C. Anthony, 2002, *American Journal of Epidemiology* 15:918-925.

Waldron H. B., S. Kern-Jones, C. W. Turner, T. R. Peterson, and T. J. Ozechowski, 2007, *Journal of Substance Abuse Treatment* 32:133-42.

Watts M., 2007, *British Journal of Nursing*, 16:1396–1398.

Woody G., S. A. Poole, G. Subramaniam, K. Dugosh, M. Bogenschutz, P. Abott, A. Patkar, M. Publicker, K. McCain, J. S. Potter, R. Forman, V. Vetter, L. McNicholas, J. Blaine, K. G. Lynch, and P. Fudala, 2008, *Journal of the American Medical Association* 300:2003–2011.

NOTES

1. WHY ADOLESCENT SUBSTANCE USE IS A BIG DEAL

1. www.monitoringthefuture.org
2. http://www.monitoringthefuture.org//pubs/monographs/mtf-overview2013.pdf
3. Ibid.
4. http://ns.umich.edu/new/releases/22362-college-students-use-of-marijuana-on-the-rise-some-drugs-declining
5. Ibid.
6. Ibid.
7. Ibid.
8. http://www.youtube.com/watch?v=RSDnLSU3owc
9. Siegel, 2014, *Brainstorm: The Power and Purpose of the Teenage Brain.*
10. Grant and Dawson, 1997, *Journal of Substance Abuse* 9:103–10.
11. Grant and Dawson, 1998, *Journal of Substance Abuse* 10:163–73.
12. Grant and Dawson, 1997, *Journal of Substance Abuse* 9:103–10.
13. Grant and Dawson, 1998, *Journal of Substance Abuse* 10:163–73.
14. Casey et al., 2008, *Development Review* 28:62–77.
15. 1969 draft report "Why One Smokes" to the Philip Morris board of directors. Document Bates No. 1003287836.
16. A 1973 RJR draft paper, "Some Thoughts about New Brands of Cigarettes for the Youth Market." Bates No 502987357-7368.
17. 1980 report, "Apparent Difficulties and Relevant Facts." Bates No. 689753864.

18. 1970 (August 13) message from a Lorillard advertising account executive to a marketing professor, soliciting help from his students with advertising design. Bates No. 92352889.

19. Counotte et al., 2011, *Developmental Cognitive Neuroscience* 1:430–43.

20. Counotte et al., *2012 Frontiers in Pharmacology* 3:1–6.

21. Beal et al., 2013, *Prevention Science* 15:506–15.

22. http://www.tobaccofreekids.org/content/what_we_do/industry_watch/product_manipulation/2014_06_19_DesignedforAddiction_web.pdf

23. "Tobacco Use Epidemic in the U.S.: Is 50 Years of Progress Enough?" http://www.surgeongeneral.gov/initiatives/tobacco/.

24. Coleman et al., 2014, *Pharmacology Biochemistry and Behavior* 116:142–51.

25. Gass et al., 2014, *Neuropsychopharmacology* 9:117–25.

26. Jacobus et al., 2013, *Psychiatry Research* 214:374–81.

27. Squeglia et al., 2014, *Developmental Cognition and Neuroscience* 9:117–25.

28. Fernandez-Ruiz et al., 2004, *Neurotoxicity Research* 6:389–401.

29. Jager and Ramsey, 2013, *Current Drug Abuse Review* 1:114–23.

30. Rubino et al., 2009, *Hippocampus* 19:763–72.

31. Meier et al., 2012, *Proceedings of the National Academy of Sciences* 109:E2657-64.

32. Meier et al., 2013, *Proceedings of the National Academy of Sciences USA* 12:E980-82.

33. Hall and Degenhardt, 2009, *Lancet* 374:1383–91.

34. Degenhardt et al., *Addiction* 108:124–33.

35. Fergusson et al., 2006, *Addiction* 101:556–69.

36. Smith, M. J. et al., 2015, *Hippocampus*.

37. Gilman, J. M., et al., 2014 *The Journal of Neuroscience* 34:5529–5538.

38. Hall and Lynskey, 2005, *Drug and Alcohol Review* 24:39–48.

39. Degenhardt et al., 2010, *Drug and Alcohol Dependence* 108:84–97.

40. Ibid.

41. Elvis Duran on the Z100 Morning Show on Friday, November 8, 2013.

42. Rhee et al., 2003, *Archives of General Psychiatry* 60:1256–64.

43. Dickson et al., 2014, *Addiction Biology* 19:37–48.

44. Solinas et al., 2004, *Neuropsychopharmacology* 29:1301–11.

45. Wagner and Anthony, 2002, *American Journal of Epidemiology* 15:918–25.

46. Brown et al., 1996, *Journal of Studies on Alcohol and Drugs* 57:314–24.

47. Crowley and Riggs, 1995, NIDA Research Monograph 156:49–111.

48. Mokdad et al., 2004, *Journal of the American Medical Association* 291:1238-45.

49. ASCD, 2012, Making the Case for Educating the Whole Child,http://www.wholechildeducation.org/assets/content/mx-resources/WholeChild-MakingTheCase.pdf

50. Fergusson et al., 2006, *Addiction* 101:556–69.

51. Silins et al., 2014, *Lancet Psychiatry*, 10.1016/S2215-0366(14)70307-4

52. Everett et al., 1999, *Accident Analysis and Prevention* 31:667–73; Hendershot et al. 2010, *Psychology of Addictive Behavior* 24:404–14.

53. NHTSA (2008), http://www-nrd.nhtsa.dot.gov/Pubs/811169.PDF

54. Thurstone et al., 2013, *American Journal on Addiction* 22:558–65.

55. Amy Weiland interview, September 8, 2014.

2. PARENTS' TOOLS FOR PLANNING, COMMUNICATING, AND MONITORING

1. Interview, September 17, 2014.

2. Interview, September 16, 2014.

3. Johnston et al., 2014, http://www.monitoringthefuture.org//pubs/monographs/mtf-vol1_2013.pdf.

4. Johnston et al. 2014.

5. Johnston et al., 2014.

6. Interview, September 17, 2014.

7. Interview, September 17, 2014.

8. http://www.sciencedaily.com/releases/2014/06/140627133057.htm

9. Interview, September 17, 2014.

10. http://www.accessdata.fda.gov/scripts/cdrh/cfdocs/cfIVD/Search.cfm

3. WHAT TO DO WHEN YOU LEARN YOUR CHILD IS USING DRUGS

1. Watts, 2007, *British Journal of Nursing*, 16:1396–1398.

2. Rosenberg, 2003, *Nonviolent Communication: A Language of Life.*

3. Siegel, 2014, *Brainstorm: The Power and Purpose of the Teenage Brain.*

4. WHEN TO SEEK TREATMENT AND WHAT TO LOOK FOR IN IT

1. Hall and Degenhardt, 2009, *Lancet* 374:1383–91.

2. http://www.drugabuse.gov/publications/seeking-drug-abuse-treatment-know-what-to-ask/introduction

3. Dennis et al., 2004, *Journal of Substance Abuse Treatment* 27:197–213.

4. American Academy of Child and Adolescent Psychiatry, 2005, *Journal of the American Academy of Child and Adolescent Psychiatry* 44:609–21.

5. Klein, 2010, University of Rhode Island Inventory for Change Assessment and Substance Treatment Outcomes, oral presentation at the annual meeting of the American Academy of Child and Adolescent Psychiatry.

6. Waldron et al., *Journal of Substance Abuse Treatment* 32:133-42.

7. Riggs et al., 2004, *Journal of the American Academy of Child and Adolescent Psychiatry* 43:420–429.

8. Riggs and Davies, 2004, *Journal of the American Academy of Child and Adolescent Psychiatry* 41:1253–55.

9. Dennis et al., 2004, *Journal of Substance Abuse Treatment* 27:197–213.

10. O'Brien et al., 2004, *Biological Psychiatry* 56:703–13.

11. American Academy of Child and Adolescent Psychiatry, 2005, *Journal of the American Academy of Child and Adolescent Psychiatry* 44:609–21.

12. National Institute on Drug Abuse, 2012, *Principles of Drug Abuse Treatment.*

13. Thurstone et al., 2010, *Journal of the American Academy of Child Adolescent Psychiatry* 49:573–82.

14. reference

15. reference

16. Riggs et al., 2007, *Archives of Pediatric and Adolescent Medicine* 161:1026–34.

17. Riggs et al., 2011, *Journal of the American Academy of Child and Adolescent Psychiatry* 50:903–14.

18. Woody et al., 2008, *Journal of the American Medical Association* 300:203–11.

19. Vestal-Labrode et al. 2014, *Developmental Neuroscience* 36: 409.

20. Gray et al., 2012, *American Journal of Psychiatry* 169:805–12.

21. Liddle and Rowe, 2010, *Adolescent Substance Abuse Research and Clinical Advances.*

22. Miller and Rollnick, 2012, *Motivational Interviewing.*

5. SPECIFIC FAMILY OBJECTIVES DURING TREATMENT

1. Kumpfer et al., 2004, *Substance Use and Misuse* 39:671–98.

2. Ibid.

3. Baumrind, 1993, *Child Development* 64:1299–317.

4. Hoeve et al., 2009, *Journal of Abnormal Child Psychology* 37:749–75.

5. Bandura, 1978, *Journal of Communication* 28:12–29.

6. Skinner, B. F., *Science and Human Behavior*, 1965.

7. Kumpfer et al., 2004, *Substance Use and Misuse* 39:671–98.

8. Cabrera et al., 2000, *Child Development* 71:127–36.

9. Hoeve et al., 2009, *Journal of Abnormal Child Psychology* 37:749–75.

10. Kumpfer et al., 2004, *Substance Use and Misuse* 39:671–98.

11. Bennett et al., 1988, *British Journal of Addiction* 83:821–29.

12. Bandura, 1978, *Journal of Communication* 28:12–29.

13. Alati et al., 2014, *Drug and Alcohol Dependence* 134:178–84.

14. Kandel et al., 2001, *Parental influences on adolescent marijuana use and the Baby Boom Generation: Findings from the 1979-1996 National Household Surveys on Drug Abuse*, Substance Abuse and Mental Health Services Administration.

15. Kumpfer et al., 2004, *Substance Use and Misuse* 39:671–98.

16. Simons-Morton, 2004, *Addictive Behavior* 29:299–309.

17. Johnston et al., 2014, Monitoring the Future national survey results on drug use 1975-2013 Volume I secondary school students.

18. Beardslee and Podorefsky, 1988, *American Journal of Psychiatry* 145:63–69; Kumpfer et al., 2004, *Substance Use and Misuse* 39:671–98.

19. Kumpfer et al., 2004, *Substance Use and Misuse* 39:671–98.

20. Ibid.

6. SPECIFIC FAMILY OBJECTIVES DURING SESSION

1. www.ucdenver.edu/encompass

2. Kumpfer et al., 2004, *Substance Use and Misuse* 39:671–98.

3. Rosenberg, 2003, *Nonviolent Communication: A Language of Life*.

4. Meek Publishing, 2011, *Parent to Parent*.

5. www.ucdenver.edu/encompass

7. HOW PARENTS CAN HELP THEIR ADOLESCENTS NOT USE SUBSTANCES

1. www.tallcopsaysstop.com

8. ADDICTION IS A CHRONIC CONDITION THAT REQUIRES CHRONIC MAINTENANCE

1. Tomlinson et al., 2004, *Psychology of Addictive Behaviors*, 18:160–69.

9. TAKING CARE OF YOU

1. Cabrera et al., 2000, *Child Development* 71:127–36.
2. Hoeve et al., 2009, *Journal of Abnormal Child Psychology* 37:749–75.
3. Bandura, 1978, *Journal of Communication* 28:12–29.

10. ADVOCATING FOR ADOLESCENT SUBSTANCE PREVENTION

1. National Survey on Drug Use and Health, http://www.samhsa.gov/data/NSDUH/2012SummNatFindDetTables/Index.aspx.
2. Riggs et al., 2007, *Archives of Pediatric and Adolescent Medicine* 161:1026–34.
3. Riggs et al., 2011, *Journal of the American Academy of Child and Adolescent Psychiatry* 50:903–14.
4. Thurstone et al., 2010, *Journal of the American Academy of Child and Adolescent Psychiatry* 49:573–82.
5. Treatment Episode Data Set, 2009, http://wwwdasis.samhsa.gov/teds07/TEDSHigh2k7.pdf
6. Dennis et al., 2004, *Journal of Substance Abuse Treatment* 27:197–213.
7. O'Brien et al., 2004, *Biological Psychiatry* 56:703–13.
8. American Academy of Child and Adolescent Psychiatry, 2005, *Journal of the American Academy of Child and Adolescent Psychiatry* 44:609–21.
9. National Institute on Drug Abuse, 2012, *Principles of Drug Abuse Treatment.*
10. Newsweek, 2012. The New Pot Barons: Businessmen bank on marijuana. http://www.thedailybeast.com/newsweek/2012/10/21/will-pot-barons-cash-in-on-legalization.html.
11. Chen et al., 1995, *American Journal of Public Health* 85:41–47.
12. Hall and Degendardt, 2009, *Lancet* 374:1383–91.
13. National Survey on Drug Use and Health.
14. Rabinoff, 2006, *Ending the Tobacco Holocaust.*
15. Walton et al., 2014, *Nicotine and Tobacco Research.*
16. Ibid.

17. Ibid.

18. Ibid.

19. Centers for Disease Control and Prevention, 2013, Tobacco Product Use Among Middle and High School Students—United States 2011–2012.

20. Jawad et al., 2013, *Addiction* 108:1873-1884; Klein et al., 2008, *Nicotine and Tobacco Research* 10:1209–14).

21. Charlesworth and Glantz, 2005, *Pediatrics*, 116:1516–28.

22. Garnder and Brandt, 2006, *American Journal of Public Health* 96:222–32.

23. Gordon et al., 2013, *Current Psychiatry Report* 15:419.

24. Hall and Degenhardt, 2009, *Lancet* 374:1383–91.

25. Luke and Krauss, 2004, *American Journal of Preventive Medicine* 27:362–72.

26. http://www.cnbc.com/id/101886620

27. http://www.businessinsider.com/new-york-times-leafly-marijuana-ad-2014-8, Aug. 2, 2014, 9:01 PM

28. Richter and Levy, 2014, *New England Journal of Medicine*, 371:399–401.

29. Salomonsen-Sautel et al., 2012, *Journal of the American Academy of Child and Adolescent Psychiatry* 51:694–702.

30. Thurstone et al., 2011, *Drug and Alcohol Dependence* 118:489–92.

31. Thurstone et al., 2013, *Journal of the American Academy of Child and Adolescent Psychiatry* 52:653–54.

32. Salomonsen-Sautel et al., 2014, *Drug and Alcohol Dependence* 140:137–44.

33. Schuermeyer et al., 2014, *Drug and Alcohol Dependence* 140:145–55.

34. Johnson et al. www.monitoringthefuture.org.

35. Johnson et al. www.monitoringthefuture.org.

12. SUMMARY

1. Prochaska et al., 2004, *Journal of the American Medical Association* 72:11441156.

2. Gray et al., 2011, *Drug and Alcohol Dependence* 117:242–247.

INDEX

A Better High, 142
academic achievement, 15, 26, 53, 103
Adderall, 3
Al-Anon, 40, 80, 115, 122, 129, 141
Alcohol: abstinence, 83; access, 21; as
   gateway drug, 13–15; brain
   development, 6–8, 11, 145–146;
   commercialization, 4, 16, 133, 149;
   communication, 23–24, 25–27, 33, 45,
   51; dependence, 6, 19, 54, 98; in
   home, 83, 84, 102; monitoring use, 21,
   33–34, 40, 53, 59; parental use, 83;
   social norms, 4–8, 37; support, 115;
   teen use, 1, 137; treatment, 68; use
   prevention, 137, 142
Alcoholics Anonymous,. *See also* Al-Anon,
   Nar-Anon 97, 112, 113, 122, 148
allowance, 91, 101
American Academy of Child and
   Adolescent Psychiatry, 57, 59
American Academy of Pediatrics, 59
American Tobacco, 135
amygdala, 6
anger, 40, 62, 74–75, 82, 84, 121, 146
anxiety, 12, 53, 56, 57, 62, 65, 121, 147
Attachment Communication Training
   (ACT), 41, 95
Attachment Treatment and Training
   Institute, 41–48
attention deficit disorder (ADD), 10, 12,
   66

attention deficit hyperactivity disorder
   (ADHD), 65, 67, 135. *See also*
   Adderall
authoritaran parents, 74
automobile, 16, 103
Azevedo, Josh, 25, 117, 141

behavior changes, 11, 30
behavioral control, 75
Bellace, Matt, 142
Big Tobacco, 9, 135, 136
binge drinking, 1, 11, 83
blood test, 34
Blue Book, 97–98
body spray, 30, 106
Boise, Idaho, Police Department,
   104–105
Bonavitacola, Father John, 19–20, 30, 33,
   77, 100, 108, 118, 137, 141
brain development, 5–7, 11, 12, 49, 145
Brainstorm: The Power and Purpose of
   the Teenage Brain, 139
Brown & Williamson, 9
bubblegum, 107
Buprenorphine, 67

Campaign for Tobacco-Free Kids, 10
case management, 140
Centennial, Colorado. *See* Cornerstone
   Program
cerebellum, 6

cigarettes: filters,. *See* tobacco, nicotine
11
clergy, 60
clinician, selection, 57–58
clothing, 104–105
co-occurring disorder, 15, 66
cocaine, 14
cognitive behavioral therapy, 56, 140
Colorado Springs. *See* McGuire
communication: parent-child, 21, 22–26,
41–48, 74, 91, 93–96
Community Anti-Drug Coalitions, 142
contingency management, 140
control, 40, 41, 45, 48–51, 59, 66, 73,
75–84, 109, 111, 120–122, 122, 142
cooccurring psychiatric disorder, 56, 65
coordination, drug effect on, 11
Cornerstone Program, 75–76, 100–101,
120, 126, 141
CounterDrug Task Force, 142
Covey, Stephen, 91
Crossroads Program,. *See also* Szachta,
Frank 16, 98
curfew, 28, 33, 35, 44, 47, 62, 76, 94

dabbing, 107
David, Steven H., 27
dependence, 6, 11
depression, 10, 53
detachment, 80
discipline, 74–75, 76
discussion questions, 17
discussion questions, 17, 38, 51, 70, 88,
98, 110, 128, 138
Disulfiram, 68
driving, 6, 33, 53, 103, 109, 135, 136
Drug and Alcohol Testing Industry
Association (DATIA), 35
drug paraphernalia, 53, 62, 106, 107, 136,
137, 146
drug screening, 33, 34, 35–36, 140

e-cigarettes, 134
earned high, 26, 142
ecstasy, 63
education, drug use by level of, 3
empathy, 73, 111
enabling, 73, 75, 78, 100, 101–103, 107,
121, 123, 148

Encompass, 90–93, 141
Enthusiastic Sobriety Approach, 141
Evergreen, Colorado. *See* Attachment
Treatment and Training Institute
experimentation, 20, 54
extended family, 87
extinction burst, 107

Facebook, 109, 130, 139
family therapy, 89
family treatment, 56, 140
fear, 4, 29, 33, 36, 39, 40, 71, 75–76, 85,
100, 112, 121
feedback, 33, 42, 46, 79
Food and Drug Administration U.S.
(FDA), 35, 67, 134, 163n14
Frank Szachta, 75–76, 83–84, 85–86, 87,
97–98, 100–101, 108, 120, 126, 141
Full Circle, 19

gateway drugs, 12–15, 54, 62
gender, drug use by, 3
goal-setting, 87
ground rules: communication, 41–42
guilt, 28, 39–40, 57, 75, 146

hash oil, 107
heroin, 14, 63, 64, 67, 68
hippocampus, 12
hookah bars, 135
household chores, 122
houusehold contribution, 86–87, 92

impulsivity, 10
integrated treatment, 56, 65, 140
intensive outpatient treatment, 66
IOGT International, 143
IQ, 12

Jermaine Galloway, 104–105, 107
Joe G., 36–37, 54–55, 96, 109, 112, 124,
131
Johnston, Lloyd, 2

Kennedy, Patrick J., ix, 143

Lady Gaga, 14
Lancet Psychiatry, 15
lawyer, 103

learning, alcohol effect on, 11
Let go, and let God, 122
Level 2 / Level 3 treatment, 66
Levy, Terry M. 41, 48
listening skills, 44–45
Lorillard, 9
lunch money, 101

marijuana: addiction, 59;
    commercialization, 4, 134–136, 145,
    149; daily use, 2, 3; in household, 45,
    106; in media, 31; legalization, 132,
    133, 143; monitoring use, 47, 51, 63,
    107; parental use, 25, 83; products,
    107; treatment, 68; use, 2–3, 6, 10,
    11–16, 54, 59, 63, 126, 136
maturation. *See* brain development
McGuire, Jo, 31, 35, 51, 72, 103, 105, 113,
    121
media, 4, 16, 21, 31, 50, 103, 132, 136
Media Salad Inc., 171
medication-assisted treatment, 140
memory, 11, 12
mental health, ix–x, 53, 56, 57, 59, 60, 63,
    64, 69, 90, 103, 106, 121, 126, 140,
    141, 147
Mental Health Parity and Addiction
    Equity Act (MHPAEA), ix
Methylphenidate, 67
Minuchin, Salvador, 141
mobile phones, 27, 31, 101
monitoring child behavior, 26–29, 32–36,
    51
Monitoring the Future,, 1–3
motivation, 12
motivational interviewing, 140
music, 31

N-acetylcysteine, 68
naloxone, 67
Naltrexone, 68
Nar-Anon, 115
National Association of Drug Court
    Professionals, 143
National Drug and Alcohol Research
    Center (Australia), 15
National Institute on Alcohol Abuse and
    Alcoholism, 139

National Institute on Drug Abuse
    (NIDA), 56–57
National Institute on Drug Abuse, 1, 139,
    142
National Institute on Drug Abuse, 4
National Registry of Evidence-Based
    Practices and Programs (NREPP), 60
National Registry of Evidence-Based
    Programs and Practices, 139
National Survey on Drug Use and Health,
    13
Natural High Education Network, 142
neglect, 75
Nell C., 50, 63–64, 112
New England Journal of Medicine, 136
nicotine, 9–11, 14
Nonviolent Communication: A Language
    of Life, 92, 141
nonviolent communication: A Language
    of Life, 93–95
Nucleus Acumbens, 6

Office of National Drug Control Policy,
    142
One Mind, ix
Michael, Orlans, 41
OROS, 67
Our Lady of Mount Carmel Parish, 19,
    108, 141

Parent to Parent, 141
parental drug use, 24–25
Partnership for Drug-Free Kids, 143
passive parents, 74
patience, 71
permissiveness, 100–101
Philip Morris, 9
Phoenix, Arizona. *See* The Pathway
    Program
positive relationships, 99, 113–114, 117,
    119, 122, 123, 124, 142, 147
post-traumatic stress disorder (PTSD), 66
potency, 16
praise, 33
prayer, 122, 137
prefrontal cortex, 6
prescription drugs, 3, 6, 67, 68, 107, 111,
    145
presmokers, 8

privacy, 33, 34
problem solving, 96–97
prosocial activities, 102
protective or resiliency factors, 72
psychosis, 12, 57
punishmenbt, 76

R. J. Reynolds, 9
Raymond N., 17, 32, 62
recovery insights, 17, 32, 36, 50, 54, 96,
    104, 109, 112, 124, 131
recovery programs, 57
recovery protection plan, 114–117
Reefer Sanity: Seven Great Myths of
    Marijuana, 143
reinforcement, 56, 76, 76–77
reinforcement, 76
relapse, 26, 53, 56, 67, 91, 100, 111–114,
    116, 117–118, 131, 147–148
residential treatment, 66
reverse roles, 47
Riggs, Dr. Paula, 65, 90
Rino S., 90, 103
risky behaviors, 15, 16
Robinson, Lori, 58–59
Rosenberg, Marshall, 92, 93, 141
rules, 84–86, 101
Rules for Parenting, 27

Sabet, Kevin, 143
saliva in drug test, 34, 35
self-care, 80–81, 119–123
self-driven behavior, 56
self-esteem, 71–72
7 Habits of Highly Effective People , 91
Seventh-Day Adventist, 69
shame, 41, 62, 132
sharing skills, 43–44
siblings, 28, 97–98, 102, 124–127
Siegel ,David, 139
Smart Approaches to Marijuana, 143
social hosts, 84
social media, 31, 76, 109, 130, 139
social pressure, 16, 21–22, 27

Starr S., 113
Substance Abuse and Mental Health
    Services, 60
synthetic cannabinoids, 34

Tatum, Christine, 171
Taylor, Lisa, 51, 66, 93
television, 20
Tempe, Arizona, 19
Tetrahydrocannabinol. See THC
That '70s Show, 31
THC, 12
The Kennedy Forum, ix
The Pathway Program, 25, 117, 141
third-party-payer, 132–133
Thurstone, Dr. Christopher, x, 65, 87,
    139–140, 143, 171
Timmerman, Julia, 69
Tobacco: additives, 10; as gateway drug,
    13–14, 54, 62; brain development,
    10–11, 39; commercialization, 4, 8–9,
    133–136, 149; communication about,
    23–25; companies, 8–9; parental use,
    21, 83; teen use, 2, 148
twins, 14
Twitter, 31

U.S. Surgeon General, 11
University of Colorado, 65
University of Michigan, 1
urine test, 34, 35, 140

vaporizer, 107
Volkow, Dr. Nora, 4

Washington University, 31
Weiland., Amy, 16, 112, 125, 141. See also
    Crossroads Program
Weiland, Mike, 20, 97, 102, 106–107, 141.
    See also Crossroads Program
World Federation Against Drugs, 143

Young Life, 64

ABOUT THE AUTHORS

Christian Thurstone, MD, is board certified in general, child and adolescent, and addiction psychiatry. He is medical director of a busy adolescent substance treatment program and an associate professor of psychiatry at the University of Colorado, Denver, where he researches adolescent addiction and also serves as a training director for the addiction psychiatry fellowship program. Dr. Thurstone also currently serves as a physician for the National Football League and is a past president of the Colorado Child and Adolescent Psychiatric Society. In 2012, he was awarded the White House Advocate in Action award for his efforts to reduce drug use and its consequences. That same year, the United States Congress awarded him another title: U.S. Army Major. He is honored to treat American service members needing mental health care as an Army Reserves officer. Visit his website at www.drthurstone.com.

Christine Tatum is an award-winning journalist whose market research firm, Media Salad, Inc., provides business information services that help companies and nonprofit organizations stay ahead of their competitors. Her professional stops include the *Chicago Tribune*, *The Denver Post*, the (Arlington Heights, IL) *Daily Herald*, (the (Greensboro, NC) *News & Record*, and (Colorado Springs) *The Gazette*. Tatum was elected to serve as 2006–2007 national president of the Society of Professional Journalists and has been honored to teach concepts in responsible journalism around the world at the invitation of the U.S. Department of State. She frequently collaborates with her husband to produce communications designed to inform the public about substance abuse and addiction.